PHONICS WORKBOOK

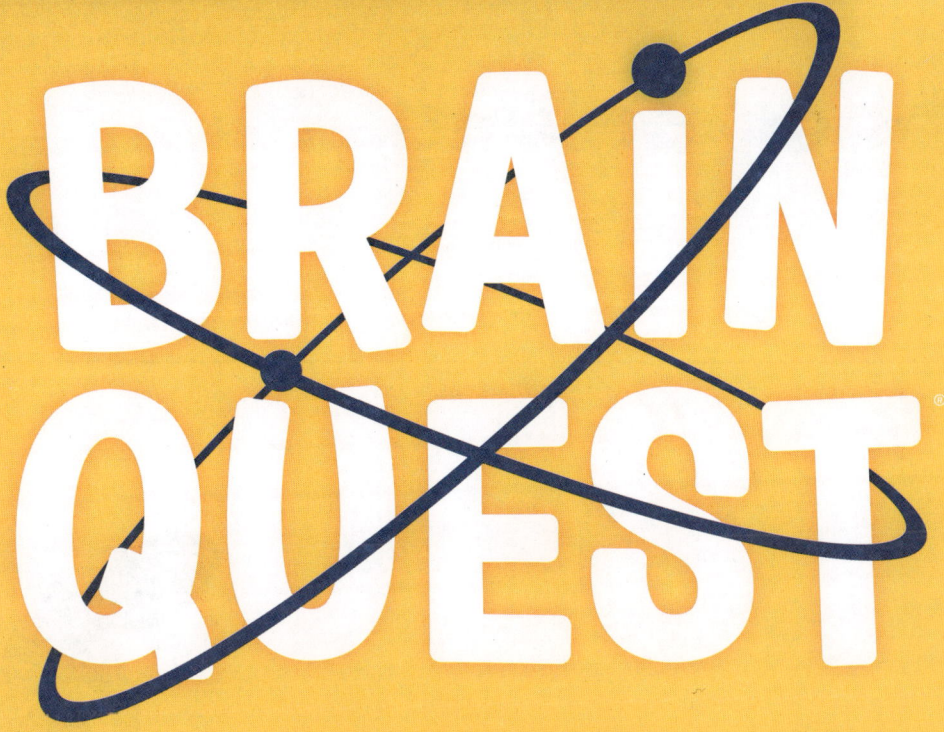

BRAIN QUEST

GRADE 2

workman

• New York •

This book belongs to:

Workman Kids
Workman Publishing
Hachette Book Group, Inc.
1290 Avenue of the Americas
New York, NY 10104
workman.com

Workman Kids is an imprint of Workman Publishing, a division of Hachette Book Group, Inc. BRAIN QUEST and the Workman name and logo are registered trademarks of Hachette Book Group, Inc.

Written by Jessica Namit
Educational Consultant: Carey Swanson
Illustrations by Jennie Bradley
Designed by Jen Keenan
Art direction by Keirsten Geise
Edited by Alisha Zucker

Workman books may be purchased in bulk for business, educational, or promotional use. For information, please contact your local bookseller or the Hachette Book Group Special Markets Department at special.markets@hbgusa.com.

ISBN 978-1-5235-2785-4

First Edition June 2025 APO
Distributed in Europe by Hachette Livre, 58 rue Jean Bleuzen, 92 178 Vanves Cedex, France.

Distributed in the United Kingdom by Hachette Book Group, UK, Carmelite House, 50 Victoria Embankment, London EC4Y 0DZ.

Printed in Shenzhen, China, on responsibly sourced paper.

10 9 8 7 6 5 4 3 2 1

DEAR PARENTS AND CAREGIVERS,

We are excited to partner with you and your child on this literacy quest! Based on the science of reading, BRAIN QUEST PHONICS WORKBOOK: GRADE 2 uses educator-vetted approaches, clear instruction, and engaging activities to help your child learn to read fluently.

Special Features

Explore these supports throughout the book with your child to enhance their learning experience:

- **Brain Boxes** support your child's learning with definitions, additional context, and pronunciation guidance.

- **Brain Quest Friends** share kid-friendly tips, explanations, and encouragement.

- **Practice Readers** provide opportunities to practice phonics concepts within the context of short, decodable stories, along with an introduction to important words to know.

Additional activities, parent tips, audiobooks for each practice reader, and more are available on BrainQuest.com.

Onward to the next chapter!

—The editors of Brain Quest

CONTENTS

Hi! My friends and I appear throughout the book to share helpful tips like:

• Read aloud the words in the activities to hear the sounds more clearly.

• Ask a good reader to stay close by so they can help you say or read words.

• Pull out the practice readers and read the stories aloud.

When you see this , add a sticker on that page and on the poster in the back to celebrate your new skills.

Are you ready? Let's go!

Blend It Up

Say the word for each picture.
What beginning sounds do you hear?

bl	cr	dr
fl	sk	sl
st		

Complete each word with a **blend** from the boxes.

<u>s</u> <u>l</u> ot

__ __ ue

__ __ um

__ __ ib

__ __ y

__ __ unk

__ __ ug

__ __ ed

BRAIN BOX

When two or more consonants are next to each other and they each make their own sound, it is called a **blend**. When you say **skip**, you can hear the **/s/** and **/k/** sounds blending together.

__ __ em

__ __ end

Two-Consonant Blends

More Blends

Say the word for each picture.
What beginning sounds do you hear?

Complete each word with a **blend** from the boxes.

cr	dr	fl
fr	pl	st
sw	tr	

__ __ an

__ __ ag

__ __ ab

__ __ og

__ __ ess

__ __ uck

__ __ op

__ __ ug

__ __ ar

__ __ im

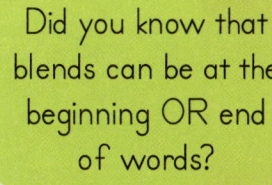

Did you know that blends can be at the beginning OR end of words?

Brain Quest Phonics Workbook: Grade 2

Two-Consonant Blends

Phone a Chicken

Say the word for each picture. Complete each word with a digraph from the colored boxes. Draw a line from each picture to the matching digraph.

c h air

30

__ __ irty

sh
wh
ch
th
ph

__ __ isker

__ __ one

__ __ ell

__ __ icken

Digraphs

A Ship and a Whale

Say the name of each picture out loud. Fill in the missing letters with a digraph from the colored boxes.

ph **sh** **th** **wh**

__ __ale

fi__ __

__ __umb

__ __ip

Remember: **ph** makes the **/f/** sound, like in **fun**.

too__ __

__ __oto

Digraphs

Blend at the End

Say the word for each picture.
Circle the ending sound you hear.

Complete each word with a blend or digraph from the boxes.

ri _ng_   (ng) ch

ben __ __   ch ck

te __ __   nd nt

lun __ __   ck ch

clo __ __   ck nk

sti __ __   nk nd

i __ __   nk nt

pea __ __   nk ch

Piggy Sort

Read the words on the coins.

Write the words on the piggy bank with the matching final blend.

blend   fund   rich   pint   king   bank

zing   song   pink   want   luck

pinch   wand   cent   dunk

rock   pick

nd — blend

ch

ck

ng

nk

nt

Brain Quest Phonics Workbook: Grade 2

Words to Know

Say each letter out loud as you color in the high-frequency words **don't**, **found**, **says**, and **your**. Read each word out loud and write it a few times on the lines below.

Don't is a **contraction** of **do not** and it contains a mark called an **apostrophe**.

don't

don't don't don't _____

found

_____

says

_____

your

_____

Circle the words **don't**, **found**, **says**, and **your** in the puzzle.

R	S	A	Y	S
I	B	Y	T	O
D	D	O	N	T
F	O	U	N	D
U	F	R	U	S

BRAIN BOX

High-frequency words are words you see a lot when reading. Pay attention to the sound and spelling of high-frequency words. Sometimes they don't follow the usual spelling.

High-Frequency Words

Ash and Liv at the Pond

Ash and Liv don't know what to do at the pond.

"We can swim," says Liv. "Do you have your swim trunks?"

"No, I don't," says Ash.

"Let me think," says Liv.

1

"Wow, Liv!" says Ash. "I found a big rock!"

"I don't think that is a big rock, Ash! You found a crab!"

Ash drops the crab.

"I want to walk back to Mom now," says Ash.
"No more crab rocks for me!"

4

"We can fish with Mom!" says Liv.
"Do you have a rod?"
"No, I don't," says Ash.
"Let me think," says Liv.

"I know! We can hunt for shells!" says Liv. "Don't you like that?"
"I do," says Ash.
Ash and Liv walk in the sand. They talk and then stop to look for shells.

Show What You Know

Why does Liv ask whether Ash brought swim trunks?

What does Ash find when he lifts the rock?

Write three words from the story that have the /sh/ sound.

Put a sticker on the poster in the back after you finish each decodable reader. Put a sticker on this page to celebrate your success in this section of the workbook!

What do you think Ash and Liv will try to do next? Draw or write about it.

PLACE STICKER HERE

Woodland Relay

We add an **-s** to the end of some verbs to show that the action is happening right now.

Add an **-s** to each word to make a new word. Then write the new word.

hop <u>s</u>   <u>hops</u>

run __   _____

nap __   _____

win __   _____

tell __   _____

chat __   _____

BRAIN BOX

A **verb** is an action word. It tells what someone or something is doing. **Run**, **play**, and **think** are all verbs.

-s Ending

Brain Quest Phonics Workbook: Grade 2

Use the picture to complete the sentences with words you wrote on page 16.

Owl _____chats_____ with Squirrel about the big race.

She _____ him all about it.

Rabbit _____ as fast as she can!

Little Deer _____ fast to keep up.

Mouse _____ near the path.

Fox _____ the race!

We don't add an **s** to a verb if "I" or "you" or more than one person is doing the action: I hop! You hop! We hop! They hop!

-s Ending

Hey, Long A!

If you say a **long a** word out loud, you can hear the name of the letter **a**, like in **paint**, **space**, or **able**.

Say the word for each picture. Circle the pictures that have a **long a** sound.

table   gray   cat   game

acorn   leaf   mail

There are different ways to spell the **long a** sound.

Circle the part of each word that makes the **long a** sound.

a **ai** **ay** **a_e** **ea** **eigh**

tray   steak   skate

baby   train   eight

Long a Spellings

Tastes Great!

Circle the words with the **long a** sound.

Then write the words on the lines.

(James) wants to make a meal.

First, he strains the pasta.

Then, he grates the cheese.

Next, he puts steak on each plate.

Last, he sets each place at the table.

Later, he has a slice of baked cake.

What a great way to end the day!

_____James_____   _____

_____   _____

_____   _____

_____   _____

_____   _____

_____   _____

Long a Spellings

I Can Find It

There are different ways to spell the **long i** sound:
i as in **kind**, **i_e** as in **bite**, **igh** as in **high**, or **y** as in **by**.

Say the word for each picture. Draw a line from the pictures with the **long i** sound to the light in the center of the page.

Sometimes when I am not sure whether a word makes a long vowel sound, I say the word and the vowel's name out loud to myself until I can figure it out.

lion

five

lime

fly

pin

smile

long i

milk

crib

right

kite

pie

ice

spider

wick

Long i Spellings

Ivy in the Library

Read these sentences out loud.
Draw a line under each **long i** word.
Circle the letters that make the **long i** sound.

 i   i_e   igh   y

Ivy is in the library.
What a sight! It is Ira.
He is right by her.

Ira says, "Hi, Mr. Simon!"
Mr. Simon sits behind a desk.
"What can I help you find?" he says.

"I like to read about science," says Ira.
Ivy says, "I like animals."
"Hmm, I have an idea," says Mr. Simon.

"Would you like to try this book?" says Mr. Simon.
"It is about spiders and butterflies."
"We like it!" say Ivy and Ira. They smile.

Write a sentence using as many of the underlined words
as you can.

_____

_____

Long i Spellings

Rhyme Time

Words that **rhyme** have the same ending sound.
Hat and **bat** rhyme—they both end with the **/at/** sound.

Read the words out loud.
Circle the words in each row that rhyme.

pie   skate   cry

 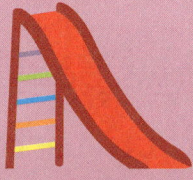 

snake   lake   tent

BRAIN BOX

Rhyming words can have the same ending sounds, like **guy** and **spy**, or they can have the same middle *and* ending sounds, like **packet** and **jacket**. Rhyming words can use different spellings to make the same sounds, like **hi** and **bye**.

ship   slide   fried

eight   child   crate

Wild Child

Read the story out loud. The missing word in each sentence rhymes with another word in the sentence.

Fill in the missing word with a word from the colored boxes. Circle the word it rhymes with.

play   hi   child   slime   might   like   hide

_____Hi_____! My name is (Skye.)

My mom says I am a wild _____.

I like to _____ all day long.

When I am outdoors, I _____ to ride my bike.

When I am inside, I play _____ and seek.

Well done! You're ready for prime time rhyme time!

One time, I made green _____.

I _____ make some more tonight.

Rhyme

Oh, Hello!

There are different ways to spell the **long o** sound: **o** as in **go**, **o_e** as in **hole**, **oa** as in **toad**, **ow** as in **low**, and **oe** as in **doe**.

Say the word for each picture. Complete the **long o** words using the letters in the colored boxes.

o   oa   oe   ow   o_e

c o a t

g __ ld

pill ___ ___

r __ s __

s ___ ___ p

b ___ ___ l

n __ s __

b ___ ___ t

b ___ ___

yell ___ ___

t ___ ___

r __ p __

Let's Go!

Read the article. Circle the words with the **long o** sound. Then write the **long o** words on the correct vowel card.

LOCAL GOAL

(Coach) throws the ball to a player on the field. Hugo runs and passes the ball to Moe. Moe shoots the ball close to the goal. The whole team shouts, "Let's go!" Then Joan kicks it in with her toe. Goal!

oa like boat

coach
_____
_____

oe like doe

_____
_____

ow like snow

_____
_____

o_e like home

_____
_____

o like open

_____
_____

Use the Unicorns

There are different ways to spell the **long u** sound: **u** as in **unit**, **u_e** as in **use**, or **ue** as in **argue**.

Say each word out loud. Draw a line between each **long u** word and the matching unicorn.

human

argue

use

music

cube

mute

unit

u_e
cute

u
unicorn

ue
hue

value

huge

menu

excuse

rescue

cue

Cute Cupid

Read each word out loud.

Underline the letter or letters that make the **long u** sound.

Then write a word from the boxes that uses the same **long u** spelling.

humor   huge   mule   rescue   music

 m<u>u</u>t<u>e</u>
mule

 argue
_____

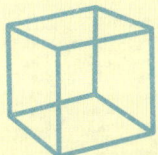 cube
_____

 cupid
_____

 human
_____

Write one more **long u** word for each spelling type.

u	u_e	ue
_____	_____	_____

Long u Spellings

Field Bunny

There are different ways to spell the **long e** sound: **e** as in **be**, **ea** as in **eat**, **ee** as in **see**, **ey** as in **key**, **e_e** as in **eve**, **ie** as in **chief**, **i** as in **ski**, and **y** as in **copy**.

Circle the letter or letters that make the **long e** sound in each word.

Match the **long e** words that have the same **long e** spelling.

beach   bee

cookie   dream

ski   field

hero   baby

turkey   taxi

feet   equal

bunny   monkey

Queen E

Read each word out loud. Circle the part of each word that makes the **long e** sound.

e ea ee ey ie y

queen

meow

seal

puppy

key

movie

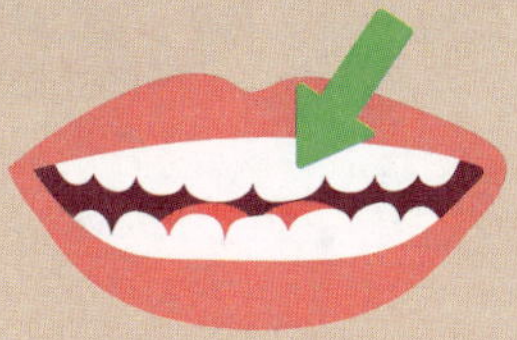

teeth

candy

beach

Great job with long vowel sounds!

Long e Spellings

Words to Know

Say each letter out loud as you color in the high-frequency words **awake**, **read**, and **work**. Read each word out loud and write it a few times on the lines below.

awake _____

read _____

work _____

Circle the correct word. Then write it on the line.

I _____ books at the library. **work** **read**

When Hank is _____ late, he uses a night-light to see. **awake** **read**

My dad likes to _____ in the garden. **awake** **work**

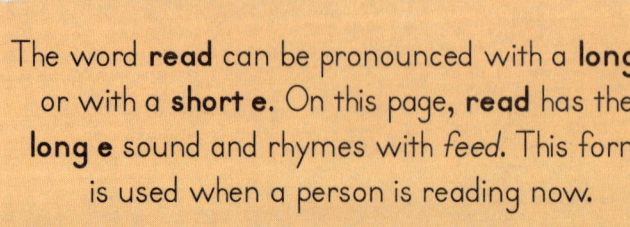

The word **read** can be pronounced with a **long e** or with a **short e**. On this page, **read** has the **long e** sound and rhymes with *feed*. This form is used when a person is reading now.

Brain Quest Phonics Workbook: Grade 2

Daytime

When I sleep and dream in bed,
I see pictures in my head.

Then I wake up to see,
that the day has come to me.

I am awake! It is a new day.
I can work, I can play.

Time to go, time to do,
time to put on my red shoes.

I find my yellow bike outside
and put on my helmet for the ride.

I pass the pool, I see green grass,
then I meet my friends in class.

After school, I like to play.
It is the best part of my day.

This is a **poem**, a type of writing that uses imaginative words to share a story, ideas, or emotions with a reader. Some poems rhyme, like this one!

Night Light

As the sun goes low,
and the eve begins to grow

I can see the soft light
that shines outside at night.

This bright moonlight
helps me see at night.

When I walk down the hall,
the moon helps me see it all.

Some say that the night
is a time of fear and fright.

Not so for me,
inside I feel happy.

Maybe you feel that too,
when you take in the nighttime view.

Do you look up at the sky,
up at the moon so very high?

At last it is time to read and rest.
I like nights like this the best.

In my bed, where I lay,
I say goodnight to another day.

Show What You Know

Answer questions about "Daytime" and "Night Light."

In "Daytime," why does the speaker say, "time to put on my red shoes"?

In "Daytime," what is the speaker's favorite part of the day?

In "Night Light," what does the speaker use to help them see?

What do you notice about the ending sounds of each pair of lines in the poems?

What do you see when you look up at the night sky?

Choose a word from either poem and write it in the smaller box. Then write as many words that rhyme with it as you can.

PLACE STICKER HERE

Florida Orange

When the letter **r** follows a vowel, it affects what sound the vowel makes. This is called an **r-controlled vowel**. The **r-controlled o** makes the **/or/** sound, like in **for**, **more**, and **torn**.

Say each word out loud.

Color the **r-controlled o** words with the **/or/** sound **orange**.

BRAIN BOX

R-controlled vowels don't make a long or short vowel sound. The **r-controlled o** makes the **/or/** sound with these letter combinations too: **ore** (more), **ar** (war), **our** (four), **oar** (roar), and **oor** (door).

Time to Roar

Read each word out loud.

Sort the words by **/or/** sound and write them below the matching colored box.

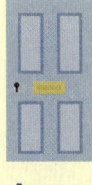 door  core  oar  four  award

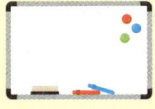 board  floor  snore   corn  score

oor
door

oar
_____

ar
_____

or
_____

ore
_____

our
_____

r-controlled o

In the Past

Adding **-ed** to the end of a verb means that the action happened in the past: I walk**ed** to the park.

Read the story out loud. Underline the verbs that end in **-s**. Rewrite the verb by adding **-ed** to the end of it to show that the action happened in the past.

Ari <u>walks</u> into his house. ___walked___

He works on his homework. _____

Then he plays with his siblings. _____

He talks with Mom. _____

He asks for pizza for dinner. _____

Ari misses his family all day. _____

A **verb** is a word that shows action. A **past tense verb** means the action already happened.

Puppy Greetings

When a verb already ends in **e**, you can just add the **d** to make it past tense.

Add **d** to these words and write the new verbs on the lines. Read the words out loud.

hope _hoped_   notice _____

love _____   wiggle _____

smile _____   excite _____

> When a word ends in a **silent e**, drop the final **e** before adding word endings that start with vowels like **–ed**, **–es**, or **–ing**.

Complete each sentence with a verb you wrote above.

Nala _____ her person very much.

She _____ Serena would get home soon.

Nala _____ someone at the door!

She _____ her body and Serena

_____ .

They were very _____ to see each other.

Past Tense Verbs

Word Treasures

R-controlled e, i, and **u** make the **/er/** sound in words like **verb**, **stir**, and **fur**.

Read the words in the colored boxes aloud.

Write each word next to the picture that has the same r-controlled vowel spelling.

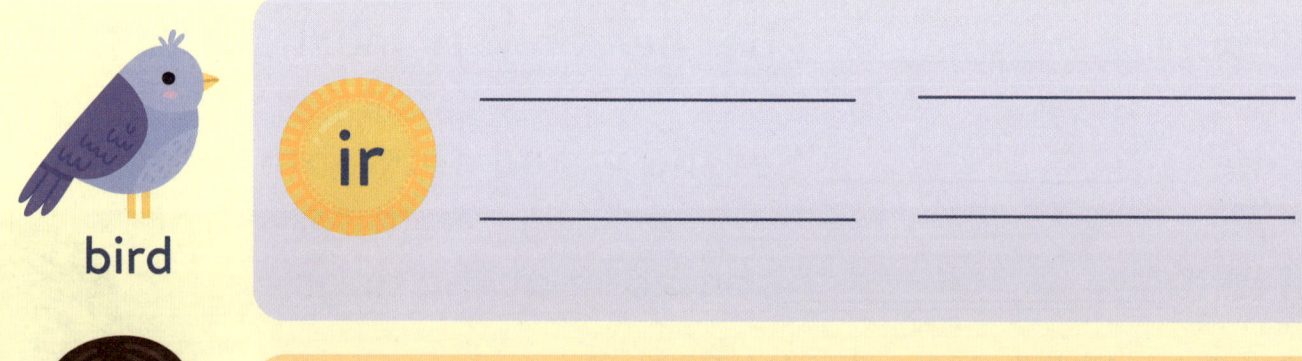

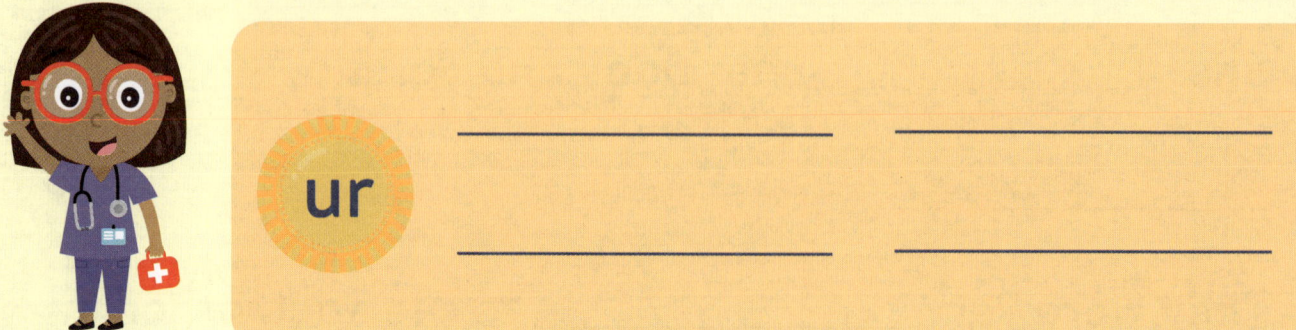

| fern | curtain | burp | surprise | stir | curb |

| chirp | spider | dirt | third | otter | over |

tiger

er ___fern___ _____

_____ _____

bird

ir _____ _____

_____ _____

nurse

ur _____ _____

_____ _____

Birds and Feathers

Read each word out loud. Circle the part of each word that makes the **/er/** sound.

Rewrite the word on the line.

 er ir ur

tu(r)tle

turtle

feather

_____

shirt

_____

ladder

_____

purse

_____

purple

_____

skirt

_____

bird

_____

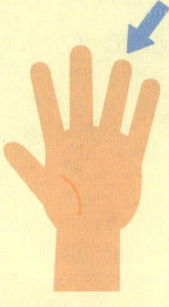

finger

_____

r-controlled vowels

Catch a Star

The **r-controlled** a makes the **/ar/** sound in words like **car**, **farm**, and **star**.

Read each word out loud. Color the stars with words that have the **/ar/** sound.

cargo

ar

Earth

part

galaxy

afar

stare

Mars

spark

orb

space

dark

planet

You deserve a gold star for your hard work!

Lark Street Yard Sale

Read the yard sale ad. Underline the words with the /ar/ sound. Then write the words on the lines below.

Lark Street Yard Sale

FOR SALE
* toys and charms
* old jars
* one harp
* cart full of yarn

*The car under the harp is NOT for sale.

_____   _____   _____

_____   _____   _____

_____   _____

r-controlled vowels

Good Night, Leo

Adding **-ing** to a verb shows that the action is happening now. **Think** becomes **thinking**.

Write the base word and add **-ing**.

walk ⟶ <u>walking</u>

look ⟶ _____

jump ⟶ _____

Look at the picture. Choose the word from the colored boxes that makes sense in the sentence. Write the word plus **-ing** on the line.

| sleep | eat | brush | read |

It's almost bedtime! Leo is _____ a snack.

Now Leo is _____ his hair.

Leo is _____ a bedtime story.

Leo is _____ in his bed. Good night, Leo!

Climbing and Crawling

Complete the chart with the missing words.

base word	+ ed	+ ing
ask	asked	asking
roll		
talk		
plant		
crawl		
climb		
travel		
finish		

Verb Tenses

Words to Know

Say each letter out loud as you color in the high-frequency words **once**, **upon**, **which**, and **would**. Read each word out loud and write it a few times on the lines below.

once _____

upon _____

which _____

would _____

Circle the words **once**, **upon**, **which**, and **would** in the puzzle.

T	A	E	W	I	W
W	H	I	C	H	O
O	R	C	H	E	U
N	G	A	V	E	L
C	U	P	O	N	D
E	F	A	S	L	E

Which Wish Will Bernice Pick?

Once upon a time, a girl named Bernice found an elf in her garden. The elf said he would grant her one wish.

Bernice gasped at the good news! She started thinking at once.

The elf frowned. "Sorry," he said. "I am new at this."

"I wish I did not find this elf," said Bernice.

The elf waved his hands. There was a puff of smoke. No more elf. No more burping dragon.

Bernice smiled. "Next time, I will watch my words!"

Bernice said, "I can wish for ice cream! I can wish for an orange skirt! I can even wish for a dragon! Which wish will I pick?"

Then the elf gave Bernice a wide smile and said, "As you wish!"

All of a sudden, there was a dragon in front of Bernice! It was wearing an orange skirt and eating an ice cream cone.

Bernice was surprised! "This is not my wish!" she said. The dragon licked the ice cream. Then it burped fire!

Bernice turned to the elf. "This dragon is burping fire! What will we do?"

Show What You Know

Answer questions about "Which Wish Will Bernice Pick?"

What happened after the elf said, "As you wish"?

Circle two words in the story that end with the letters **-ing**.

Then write them here.

What do you think Bernice means when she says she "will watch her words" next time?

Saying the story in your own words helps you remember what you read! Retell "Which Wish Will Bernice Pick?" to a stuffed animal, pet, or someone in your house.

Bernice got a wish from an elf! But the elf did not give the wish Bernice wanted. She got a fire-burping dragon instead.

PLACE STICKER HERE

Mail Day!

Sometimes two vowels together make a different sound. The letters **ai** and **ay** make the vowel sound in **mail** and **day**.

Look at the spelling of each word and read it aloud.

Write it in the correct column.

play · claim · stray · air · essay · wait · stay · clay · way · nail · brain · trail

The fancy phonics word for two vowels that make one sound is **diphthong**.

sn**ai**l

tr**ay**

play

Way to Play

Read the sentences out loud.

Circle the words with **ai** or **ay**.

(Raise) your hand if you want to play!

The main game is a relay race.

Run from the rail all the way to the pair of gray pails.

Hooray! Now let's race all day!

Write **ai** or **ay** to complete each word.

h _ay_

t _ _ l

gr _ _

tr _ _ n

p _ _ nt

spr _ _

Diphthongs

Slicing and Dicing

Adding **-ing** to a verb tells us that the action is happening now. For example: Dad is **slicing** and **dicing** in the kitchen.

Change these verbs to the **present tense** by crossing out the **silent e** and adding **-ing**.

make ~~e~~ _ing_   _making_

joke _____   _____

slice _____   _____

hide _____   _____

face _____   _____

drive _____   _____

change _____   _____

arrive _____   _____

Busy Partying

Read each verb. Show that the action is happening now by writing the verb **+ ing**. Remember to drop the final **e**!

verb	+ ing
use	using
ride	
save	
love	
take	

Circle the correct spelling of the verb.

Max is _____ a party.

havving   haveing   **having**

Max says we will be _____ cupcakes.

bakeing   **baking**   bakking

There will be lots of _____.

danceing   danccing   **dancing**

I am _____ for lots of frosting!

hoping   hopping   hopeing

Present Tense Verbs

Splish-Splash

Screw, **splash**, **spring**, and **strong** begin with **three-letter blends**.

To read a word beginning with a three-letter blend, say the sound each letter makes and then say the sounds together to blend them.

Read the words out loud. Write each word on the card with the matching blend.

strong   spray   spring   splat

stroll   split   string   scroll

sprint   splash   screen   screw

str

strong
_____
_____

spl

_____
_____

scr
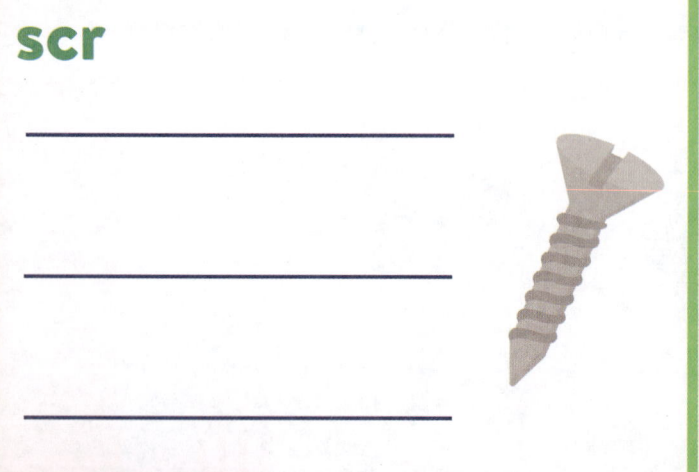
_____
_____
_____

spr
_____
_____
_____

Strawberry Blend

Pick a blend from the blender to complete the words below.

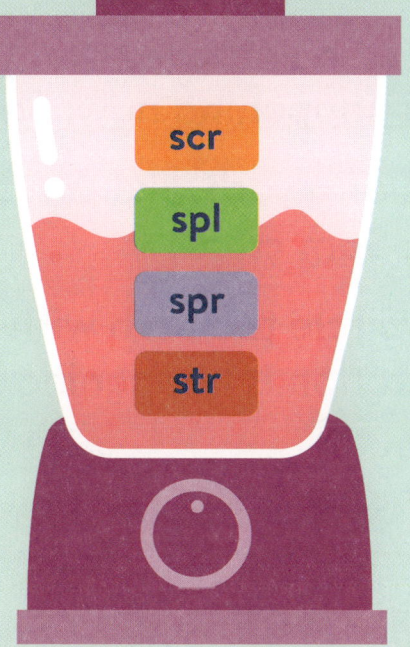

scr
spl
spr
str

Words with three-letter blends can be tricky to say. They have three consonants with no vowels between them! Practice saying each letter sound until you can blend them smoothly.

_____ipe   _____atch   _____ay

_____eet   _____aw   _____at

Three-Letter Blends

Brain Quest Phonics Workbook: Grade 2

53

Spy School

For verbs that end in **y**, change the final **y** to an **i** before adding the endings **-es** and **-ed**.

Adding **-es** to the end of a verb, like **cry**, tells that the action is happening now: Sam **cries**.

Adding **-ed** to the end of a verb, like **cry**, tells that the action happened in the past: Sam **cried**.

Read each sentence. Circle the verb with the correct ending to show whether the action is happening now or in the past.

Last night, Agent 82 **spied** **spies** some secret files.

She **copied** **copies** the files to show the other agents.

Today, Agent 82 is looking for more files. She hears a man yell, "Stop! Spy!"

She looks up and **cried** **cries**, "I am not a spy!"

Agent 82 **buried** **buries** the files in her bag and says, "I am Ms. Chan, the new teacher!"

"I am so sorry!" The man explains, "I am looking for a double agent."

Agent 82 **hurried** **hurries** toward the door. "You can never be too careful!" she shouts and walks into the night.

Now and Then

Change the verb to show that the action is happening now and in the past.

verb	now (verb + es)	past (verb + ed)
cry	cries	cried
dry		
fry		
try		

Fill in the blanks with the correct verb from the chart above.

Padme _____ to read the sheet music as she plays piano.

Ella _____ when she broke her arm.

Emily _____ jelly donuts and covers them with sugar.

Javier _____ his hands when he finished washing dishes.

Scott _____ to read, but it was too noisy in the room.

Verb Endings

So Many Things

Write a word from the colored boxes under each picture.

Add **s** to the end of the word if the picture shows more than one of each item.

bike   friend   scooter   dog   grape   swing

grapes

A **noun** names a person, place, or thing. A **plural noun** means there is more than one, usually ending in **s.**

Plural Nouns

Brain Quest Phonics Workbook: Grade 2

Kitchen Counting

If a noun ends in **s**, **x**, **z**, **ch**, or **sh**, add **-es** to make it plural.

Write the correct word below the object.
Add a final **-s** or **-es** if there is more than one.

apple   glass   pot
dish   box   table

boxes

Plural Nouns

Words to Know

Say each letter out loud as you color in the high-frequency words **should**, **something**, and **very**. Read each word out loud and write it a few times on the lines below.

should _____

something _____

very_____

Circle the correct word. Then write it on the line.

Drinking hot cocoa _____ help warm you up on a cold day. very   should

I want to teach my baby sister to say _____ funny. something   very

Bananas start out _____ green and then turn yellow as they ripen. should   very

Fun Facts About Spruce Trees

RESIN

Have you heard the saying "spruce something up"? It means to make something look cleaner and nicer. It should be no surprise, then, that spruce trees look good and smell fresh.

Spruces are very large, green pine trees. They are evergreen trees, which means they stay green all year round.

Resin is a sticky, thick goo that oozes out of spruce trees. Resin has been used for centuries to make gum, drinks, and a tar-like gloop that can be used to patch canoes or cover roofs of homes.

Spruce needles are used to make good-smelling oil, medicines, and tea. But don't try this with just any spruce trees! Check with an adult to find out which ones are safe.

Spruce trees are found in North America and other places. They grow where there is full sun, cold weather, and soil that drains well.

Spruce trees are very tall, with straight trunks. They grow in gardens, yards, and forests. They can grow as high as 100 feet tall, the length of a blue whale!

Spruce trees have many uses. Strong, light timber (wood used for building) comes from spruce trees. People have been making instruments like pianos, violins, cellos, and guitars from spruce wood for years. The wood can be used to make toys too.

Show What You Know

Answer questions about "Fun Facts About Spruce Trees."

Write two words that tell how spruce trees look.

What can be made from spruce wood?

What can be made from spruce resin?

Draw a spruce tree.

Write a verb from the text that ends in the letters -ing.

Double Bubble

When a word ends with a short vowel and then a consonant, double the last letter before adding **-ed** or **-ing**. **Zap** becomes **zapped** or **zapping**.

Circle the correct spelling of the word to complete the sentence.

Gracie was _____ a dish in the sink. **scrubing** **scrubbing**

The soap _____ into the water. **slipped** **sliped**

She tried _____ it, but it fell in. **grabing** **grabbing**

Then she _____ at all the bubbles she made! **grinned** **grined**

Double the last letter and add **-ing** or **-ed** to write a new word.

hop + ing = <u>hopping</u>   jog + ed = _____

zip + ed = _____   shop + ed = _____

beg + ing = _____   plug + ed = _____

run + ing = _____   skip + ing = _____

Popping Bubbles

Read the words and the clues to complete the puzzle.
Add **-ed** to show the action takes place in the past.
Add **-ing** to show the action takes place now. Remember
to double the last letter before adding the ending!

| clap | hug | plan | log | sob | pop | pin |

ACROSS

1. made loud noises with your hands
2. bursting bubbles
3. used a tack to hang something
4. holding tightly in your arms

DOWN

5. cried yesterday
6. cutting trees
7. deciding ahead of time

clapped

Verb Endings

Gnome Home

Some words have **silent letters**, which means we don't say that letter when we say the word. Words can have a **silent k** like in **knob**, a **silent w** like in **wrap**, a **silent g** like in **gnome**, and a **silent b** like in **comb**.

Draw lines connecting the words with silent letters to get to the gnome at the end of the maze.

know

kick

crib

wish   not

knit

gnat

wrist

crumb   knot   verb

write

sign

limb

grass

Guessing Game

Read the clues to figure out the mystery word.

| comb | gnaw | knee | knob | lamb | thumb |

This word is a noun.
It is used to keep hair neat.
The last letter is a silent b.
What is the word?

_____

This word has four letters.
It is a young animal.
The last letter is silent.
What is the word?

_____

This word is a body part.
You can put it up to show that you like something.
The last letter is silent.
What is the word?

_____

The first letter in this word is silent.
It is an action word.
It means to bite or chew something.
What is the word? _____

This word starts with a silent letter.
It is found on a door.
It is round.
What is the word?

_____

This word starts with a silent letter.
It is a body part that bends.
It is covered by pants.
What is the word?

_____

Silent Letters

Brain Quest Phonics Workbook: Grade 2

Look in the Brook

The **oo** spelling can make more than one sound.

Write the missing letters to make words that have the **/oo/** sound, as in **took**.

b o o k

f ___ t

sh ___ ___ k

w ___ ___ f

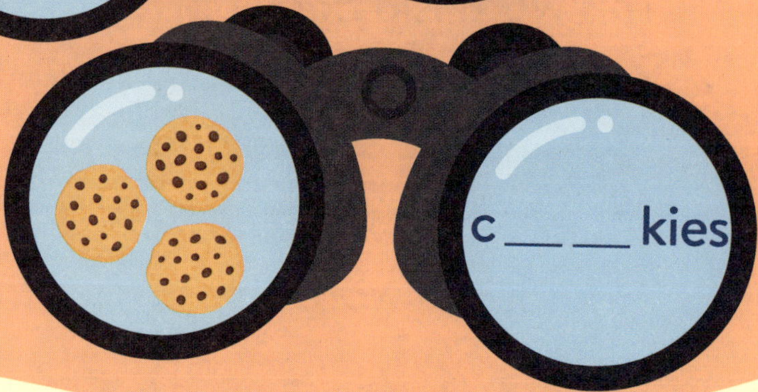

c ___ ___ kies

The word **brook** means "a small stream." When the word has a capital B, like **Brook,** it is someone's name.

HELLO MY NAME IS Brook

Read the sentences. Circle the words with the oo sound, like in rook.

Ann and Pop Pop look for fish in the brook.

Pop Pop uses a pole with a hook to catch fish.

Ann wears a coat with a wool hood.

Brain Quest Phonics Workbook: Grade 2

It's All Good

Read each definition and change one letter at a time to make a new word.

Write each new word on the line next to the definition.

cook | hood | nook | hook | look

covers the head and neck with an opening for the face

hood

a curve that can hold something

_____

glance or peek

_____

make a meal

_____

a corner or small, tucked-away area

_____

oo Words

Zooming Balloons

The letters **oo** can also make the sound heard in **zoom**. Color the balloons that show words with the **/oo/** sound, like in **balloon**.

zoo

soap

hoot

soon

honk

pool

moon

foot

tooth

plop

booth

cook

boom

took

boat

Hoops and Boots

Write a word from the colored boxes under the matching picture.

hoop	boots	tools
balloon	school	moon
goose	broom	spoon

_____   _____   _____

_____   _____   _____

_____   _____   _____

oo Words

Purple Castle

The letters **le** together at the end of a word make the ending sound heard in **purple**.

Write the words that end in **le** on the lines.

BRAIN BOX

At the beginning of **lend**, the letters **le** make two separate sounds: **/l/** and **/e/**. When **le** is at the end of a word, it makes one sound: the **/ul/** sound like in **ankle**.

able   feel   tile   bagel   leap
steer   angle   angel   gentle   towel
trouble   heal   file   tickle   title

_____able_____   _____

_____   _____

_____   _____

_____   _____

-le Ending

Word Razzle Dazzle

Add **le** to complete each word.

Then draw a line to match the word to the picture.

Write the word next to the matching picture.

hand _le_

tab __ __   _handle_ _____

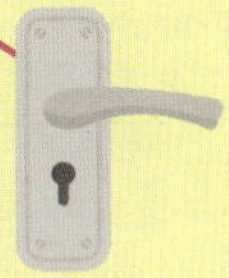

musc __ __ _____

freck __ __ s _____

cand __ __ _____

peop __ __ _____

pick __ __ _____

turt __ __ _____

Brain Quest Phonics Workbook: Grade 2

-le Ending

Let's Get Together

A **compound word** is made when two words join to become a new one. For example, the words **cup** and **cake** together become **cupcake**.

Look at the pictures to write a compound word.

 +  = <u>starfish</u>

 + ☐ = _____

 + ◯ = _____

 +  = _____

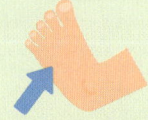 +  = _____

Use a word from each column to write a compound word.

snow	pot	_____
flash	ball	_____
flower	bowl	_____
fish	light	_____

At the Ballgame

Color the baseballs with compound words.

toothbrush

jellyfish

raccoon

carrot

footprint

ladybug

cupcake

butterfly

skateboard

bucket

robot

snowman

bathtub

popcorn

umbrella

Nice work, champ!

Brain Quest Phonics Workbook: Grade 2

Compound Words

Words to Know

Say each letter out loud as you color in **before**, **first**, and **these**. Read each word out loud and write it a few times on the lines below.

before _____

first _____

these _____

Read the clues and complete the puzzle with the words **before**, **first**, and **these**.

ACROSS

1. _____, second, third
2. plural form of *this*

DOWN

3. _____ and after

Making Sparkle Cookies

Want to dress up your cookies? You can add rainbow sprinkles to any cookies in just a few easy steps.

Before getting started, find a clean table and gather these items:

- tray
- sugar cookies
- small bowl
- spoon
- butter knife
- 1 cup powdered sugar
- 4 teaspoons milk
- rainbow sprinkles

Bring these cookies to your friends. If they like cookies with rainbow sprinkles, they will be begging to eat these! They are so good that every last crumb will be gone. Grab one while you are able to!

First, put the cookies on the tray.
Then, make the icing. Put the sugar and milk in a bowl and stir with a spoon. When you are stirring, make sure the icing is blended well so there are no chunks of sugar.

Next, spread some icing on top of one cookie. A butter knife is good for spreading the icing.

Now it is sprinkle time! Put some sprinkles on top of the icing on the cookie. Add the sprinkles right after you ice the cookie, while the icing is still wet.

Last, let the cookies sit. This helps the sprinkles stick. After the cookies have sat for one hour, they will be ready to eat!

Show What You Know

Answer questions about "Making Sparkle Cookies."

What is the first step to make sparkle cookies?

What step comes after stirring the icing?

Why should you let the cookies sit?

Write two compound words from the text here.

If you could add any topping to cookies, what would you add?

PLACE STICKER HERE

Play Time

When **f**, **l**, **s**, or **z** is at the end of a word, the letter is sometimes doubled to become **ff**, **ll**, **ss**, or **zz**. You can find this at the end of words like **puff**, **grill**, **hiss**, and **buzz**.

Write the word from the box that matches each picture.

ball   chess   doll   dress

fluff   shell   fizz

Double Up

Write a double final consonant from the colored boxes to make a word.

ff **ll** **ss** **zz**

be __ __

cli __ __

gra __ __

tro __ __

ja __ __

wa __ __

ki __ __

o __ __

Double Letters

The Juggling Rabbit

Many words have these double consonants in the middle: **bb**, **dd**, **gg**, **mm**, **nn**, **pp**, or **tt**.

The double consonants tell readers that the beginning of the word has a short vowel sound.

Circle the missing letters that complete the word. Then write the letters in the blanks and read the word out loud.

ra _b_ _b_ it

gg / **bb** / tt

hi ___ ___ o

pp / dd / mm

ha ___ ___ ock

bb / mm / tt

ju ___ ___ le

gg / dd / mm

la ___ ___ er

nn / dd / bb

ki ___ ___ en

dd / nn / tt

bb / nn / dd

pe ___ ___ y

Brain Quest Phonics Workbook: Grade 2

Apple Sort

Say each word in the colored boxes. Sort the words by double consonants on the cards below.

ribbon summer puppy minnow tennis

attic winner mammal happy wedding

muddy baggy pebble comma dribble

jiggle attend written puppet

bb
ribbon
___
___
___

dd
___
___
___

gg
___
___
___

mm
___
___
___

nn
___
___
___

pp
___
___
___

tt
___
___
___

Stormy Weather

Adding word parts to the ends of words can change their meaning. The ending **-y**, like in **watery**, means "made of." The ending **-ly**, like in **slowly**, means "in a way that is."

Add **-y** or **-ly** to the end of the words.

speed + y = <u>speedy</u>   kind + ly = _____

rock + y = _____   dry + ly = _____

smell + y = _____   even + ly = _____

Write a word from the box to complete each sentence.

<u>sunny</u> <u>mostly</u> <u>messy</u> <u>friendly</u> <u>clearly</u>

Sarah is a kind and _____ news reporter.

She _____ tells the weather, but sometimes she reads the news too.

Sarah speaks _____ on the radio.

It will rain and the roads will be _____.

It might warm up and get _____ in the afternoon.

-y and -ly Endings

Brain Quest Phonics Workbook: Grade 2

Crispy and Flaky

Complete the chart.

base word	ending	new word
smooth	+ ly	smoothly
crisp	+ y	
	+ ly	lately
trick	+ y	
	+ y	sleepy
wise	+ ly	

Write the correct word to complete each sentence.

I look out at the _____ sky.

cloudy cloudly

It is a _____ day today.

snowy snowly

Flakes fall _____.

quicky quickly

I read _____ in my room.

quiety quietly

Read **slowly** and **carefully** to catch the letter **l** that is sometimes before the letter **y** at the end of a word.

-y and -ly Endings

Time to Dismount

A **prefix** is a word part added to the beginning of a word to change its meaning. The prefix **un-** means "not," and changes **fair** to **unfair**, which means "not fair."

Sort the words below by prefix.

unlock   rebuild   replay   rename   unpack   distrust

unkind   disagree   disloyal   unwell   remix   disable

un = not

unlock

_____

_____

_____

re = again

_____

_____

_____

_____

dis = opposite of

_____

_____

_____

_____

Knowing prefixes helps me decode unfamiliar words. **Dismount** is new to me, but I know that **dis–** means the "opposite of" and **mount** means "to get on a horse." That means **dismount** is getting off a horse!

Unwrap and Unzip

Add the prefixes **un-**, **re-**, or **dis-** to the words.

Then rewrite the words.

un-

_un_ happy   _unhappy_

____ lucky   _____

____ well   _____

re-

____ play   _____

____ use   _____

____ new   _____

dis-

____ like   _____

____ honest   _____

____ respect _____

Write the meaning of each word.

unzip

rewrite

Get to the Gym!

The letter **g** makes two sounds: **hard g**, like in **get** or **frog**, and **soft g**, like in **gym** or **age**.

Sort the words onto the **hard g** or **soft g** card.

cage   game   glue   magic

log   giraffe   germ   goat

grapes   gem   dragon

hard g	soft g
game	cage

Good Oranges

Circle the word with the same **g** sound as the picture.

orange

pig page

frog

hug wedge

sponge

stage plug

mug

flag veggie

eagle

bug urge

cage

dig magic

dog

age bag

judge

range ping

bridge

angel beg

dragon

edge grow

All in All

In words like **fall**, **poll**, and **bull**, the **ll** after the vowel changes its sound.

Write a word from the colored boxes that matches each picture.

doll	call	pull	troll

waterfall	ball	gull	roll

Go All Out

Add **all**, **oll**, or **ull** to complete the words. Rewrite the words on the blanks.

sm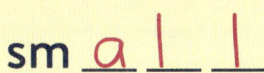

_____  _____

sk __ __ __

_____

meatb __ __ __

seag __ __ __

_____   _____

str __ __ __

unr __ __ __

_____   _____

Circle the correct word to complete the sentence.

Katie played with her favorite (**dall**, **doll**, **dull**).

Ollie ate too much candy and felt (**fall**, **foll**, **full**).

Mom said it was time to go to the (**mall**, **moll**, **mull**) to buy Bubbie a present.

Words to Know

Say each letter out loud as you color in **around**, **it's**, and **through**. Read each word out loud and write it a few times on the lines below.

around _____

it's _____

through _____

It's is a contraction of **it is**. A **contraction** is a shortened form of two words combined together.

Write a word from above to complete each sentence.

_____ never a bad day to read a book!

The plane flies _____ the clouds.

I turned _____ when I heard my name.

Carnival Buzz

Jess and I ran quickly toward the carnival gate. We could hear the buzz from outside. The yearly Bobb School Fair was finally here!

We walked through the gate and looked around. "Do you want to ride the fast coaster or the carousel first?" I asked Jess. I pointed to the animals we could sit on: tigers, giraffes, goats, and even grizzly bears.

"Please can I have a redo?" I begged the man running the game. "That prize would go great in my room," I said, pointing to the giant brown teddy bear.

"Sorry, kid. You know the rule: If you want to replay, you need to repay!" he said as he winked at us.

"Never mind, Steff!" said Jess. "You won one last year. Race you to the buggies!"

It's always a thrill to spend a day at the fair!

2

"No thanks, Steff," she said. "I disliked those rides last year. Maybe we could ride the buggies?"

As we walked past the green Putt-Putt course, I pointed out a game I really wanted to play. "Please, Jess! Can we stop here first?"

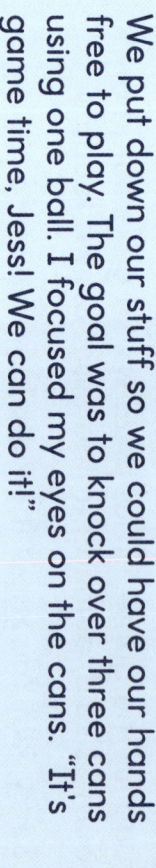

3

We put down our stuff so we could have our hands free to play. The goal was to knock over three cans using one ball. I focused my eyes on the cans. "It's game time, Jess! We can do it!"

We threw the balls as hard as we could. Jess missed the cans completely! I knocked one can down, but the other two only wobbled.

Show What You Know

Answer questions about "Carnival Buzz."

What are Jess and Steff doing for the day?

What did Jess want to do first?

What prize did Steff want to win?

Imagine you are going to a carnival or fair. What would you like to do first?

Unscramble the sentence from the story. Then rewrite it.

I toward the Jess ran gate and quickly carnival.

PLACE STICKER HERE

Plural Practice

Adding **s** or **es** to the end of a noun makes many words plural. **Irregular plurals** are words that do not follow this rule.

Write the irregular plural of the singular word.

| people | men | children | women |

Singular: One	Plural: More Than One
man	men
woman	
child	
person	

Write the correct plural in each blank.

My mom is the smartest (**woman**, **women**) I've ever met. _____

Our babysitter Bobby picks up three (**child**, **children**) after school each day.

_____

BRAIN BOX

Irregular means the word does not follow a pattern. Irregular plurals need to be memorized.

Animal Plurals

Some animal names are the same in their singular and plural forms. There is **one fish** in the sea and there are **five fish** in the lake. Notice the yellow rows— those plurals are different!

One	More Than One
deer	deer
fish	fish
goose	geese
moose	moose
mouse	mice
sheep	sheep

Underline the animal word in each sentence. Then circle whether the animal word means **one** or **more than one**.

There is a white <u>sheep</u> on the farm. (one) more than one

Three fish swim in the pond. one more than one

Two geese honk and waddle nearby. one more than one

Do you see the two deer by the fence? one more than one

A moose stands next to the tree. one more than one

There are mice on the ground! one more than one

Irregular Plurals

Lots of Loaves

To make some words that end in **f** or **fe** plural, the ending letters are replaced with **ves**.
The plural of **calf** is **calves**.
The plural of **knife** is **knives**.

Write the plural of the singular noun to complete each sentence.

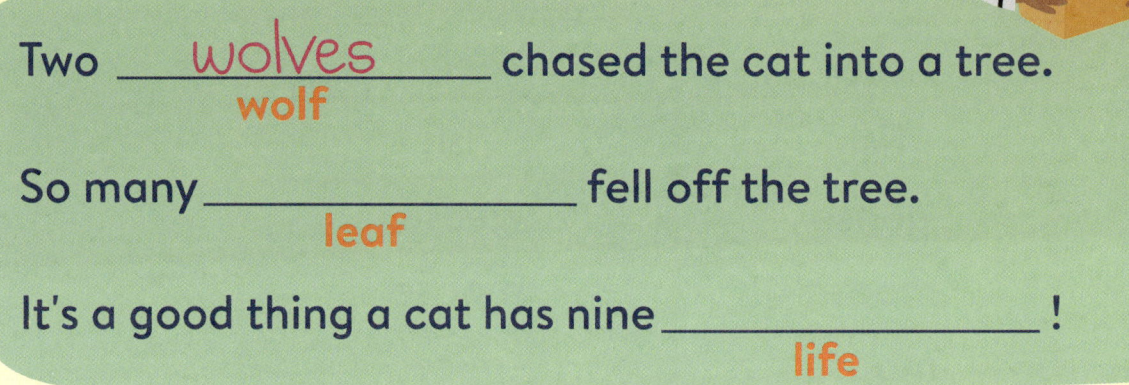

Two ____wolves____ chased the cat into a tree.
  wolf

So many_____ fell off the tree.
  leaf

It's a good thing a cat has nine_____!
  life

Baker Bob baked so many_____ of bread.
  loaf

Let's split each loaf into_____.
  half

Where are the bread_____?
  knife

The two_____ sat on the porch.
  wife

It was cold so they wore_____.
  scarf

Two baby_____grazed in their yard.
  calf

BRAIN BOX

For words that end in **ff** like **puff**, just add **s** to make them plural. For some words that end in one **f**, like **chef** or **brief**, add an **s** to create the plurals **chefs** and **briefs**.

Brain Quest Phonics Workbook: Grade 2

An Irregular Match

Match the singular word to its plural.

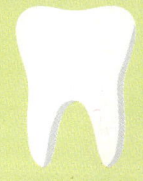

tooth

scissors

die

aircraft

shorts

jeans

aircraft

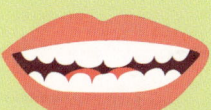

teeth

shorts

dice

jeans

scissors

Some words, like **pants**, don't have a singular form. **Pants** can mean one pair of pants or 50 pairs of pants!

Irregular Plurals

Heroes to the Rescue

When words end in **o**, add **es** to make the word plural.

Add **es** to the ends of the words below to write the plural. Then write the word.

hero _e s_

heroes

tomato __ __

_____

potato __ __

_____

echo __ __

_____

Circle the correct word to complete the sentences.

Super Sasha and the Blue Bat are the (**hero**, **heros**, **heroes**) this city needs! An evil villain nearly destroyed the market. There were (**potato**, **potatos**, **potatoes**) and (**tomatose**, **tomatoes**, **tomatos**) everywhere! Blue Bat and Super Sasha found the villain using their (**echoes**, **echos**, **echose**).

Brain Quest Phonics Workbook: Grade 2

People in the Park

Write the singular or plural forms of the missing words.

Singular	Plural
child	children
	people
	women
man	
leaf	
moose	
	wolves
mouse	
	geese
sheep	

Irregular Plurals

Full of Gum

A **suffix** is a word ending that changes the word's meaning. The suffix **-ful** means "full of." **Cheerful** means "full of cheer." The suffix **-less** means "without." **Wireless** means "without wires."

Color the words with the suffix **-ful** blue.

Color the words with the suffix **-less** yellow.

Color the other words purple.

The suffixes **–ful** and **–less** have opposite meanings. **Joyful** and **joyless** use the same base word **joy** but have opposite meanings.

beautiful · candy · amaze · endless · fruitful · handful · birds · joyful · joyless · grasp · colorless · colorful

Make New Words

Add **-ful** to the end of each word on the green gumballs and write it on the **-ful** card. Add **-less** to the end of each word on the orange gumballs and write it on the **-less** card.

play · bowl · wing · fright · price · noise · wish · bottom · law · rider

-ful

playful
_____
_____
_____
_____

-less

_____
_____
_____
_____

Suffixes

It's Cookie O'Clock

The prefix **pre-** means "before," like in **preset**.
The prefix **mis-** means "wrongly," like in **misuse**.

Circle the correct prefix.

Then write the new word on the line.

To heat before is to __*preheat*__.

To hear wrongly is to _____.

To pay before is to _____.

To spell wrongly is to _____.

Menu Mishaps

Circle the correct word to complete the sentence.
Then write the word.

Oh no! Charlotte notices a ___misprint___ in the

name of the restaurant (**misprint**, **preprint**). There

are also some _____ words (**misspelled**,

prespelled). Someone could order the wrong meal

by _____ (**mistake**, **pretake**). Charlotte

fixes the menu to _____ problems

before they happen (**misvent**, **prevent**). It's best

to _____ before the customers arrive

(**mispare**, **prepare**).

Prefixes

Words to Know

Say each letter out loud as you color in **both**, **buy**, and **enough**. Read each word out loud and write it a few times on the lines below.

both _____

buy _____

enough _____

Read the text below. Underline the words **both**, **buy**, and **enough** as you read.

I asked Grandma to buy a toy car for me.

"I don't think you will use that enough," she said.

Then I asked her to buy me some glitter.

"I don't think you will use that enough," she said.

"I promise I will use both of them, Grandma!" I said.

Grandma said, "I will buy you a T-shirt.

You will use that."

Gordon's Gardening Blog

Welcome to my blog! My name is Gordon and I am a successful gardener. In today's post, I help one of my readers with a pesky pest problem and help another reader find some sweet feet relief. Enjoy!

Dear Gordon,

Animals are eating my prize-winning potatoes and top-notch tomatoes! There are only one potato and one tomato left. How can I return my vegetable garden to the plentiful patch I once had? I feel so helpless and unhappy!

From,
Tearful and Taterless

Dear Stinky,

Kneeling and sweating are enough to make any gardener stinky! I use Gordon's Gardening Cream and I think you should too. It kills smelly foot smells. It will also help soothe your calves and feet to make gardening painless and odorless. Your shoes will thank you and so will the people around you. Buy it on my website today.

Good luck!
Gordon

Dear Tearful,

I am sorry for your misfortune. Lots of critters, like birds and mice, eat potatoes. Deer, however, like both potatoes and tomatoes. If deer don't have enough leaves to eat, they might eat your vegetables!

You can buy a scarecrow or use a fence to keep these graceful beasts out of your garden. Whether you have one or many deer, this should help.

I predict that you will have a beautiful garden again in no time!

Good luck!
Gordon

Dear Gordon,

Kneeling in my garden is painful! My feet and calves both hurt a lot! My feet are extra stinky after a full day of pruning my poppies. Got any tips to fix my body? I want to work in my flower bed, not lie in bed!

Signed,
Stinky in Springfield

Show What You Know

Answer questions about "Gordon's Gardening Blog."

Who is Gordon?

What does Gordon mean when he says, "I am sorry for your misfortune"?

What advice would you give one of the readers? Answer one of the questions in your own words.

Unscramble the sentence from the story. Then rewrite it.

my painful Kneeling is in garden.

Comparing Notes

The suffix **-er** means "more" and is used to compare two nouns. For example: Grace is **shorter** than Alisha, which means that Grace is *more short*.

The suffix **-est** means "most" and is used to compare three or more nouns. For example: Megan is the **tallest** kid in class, which means that Megan is the *most tall*.

Add **-er** or **-est** to compare nouns. Complete the chart.

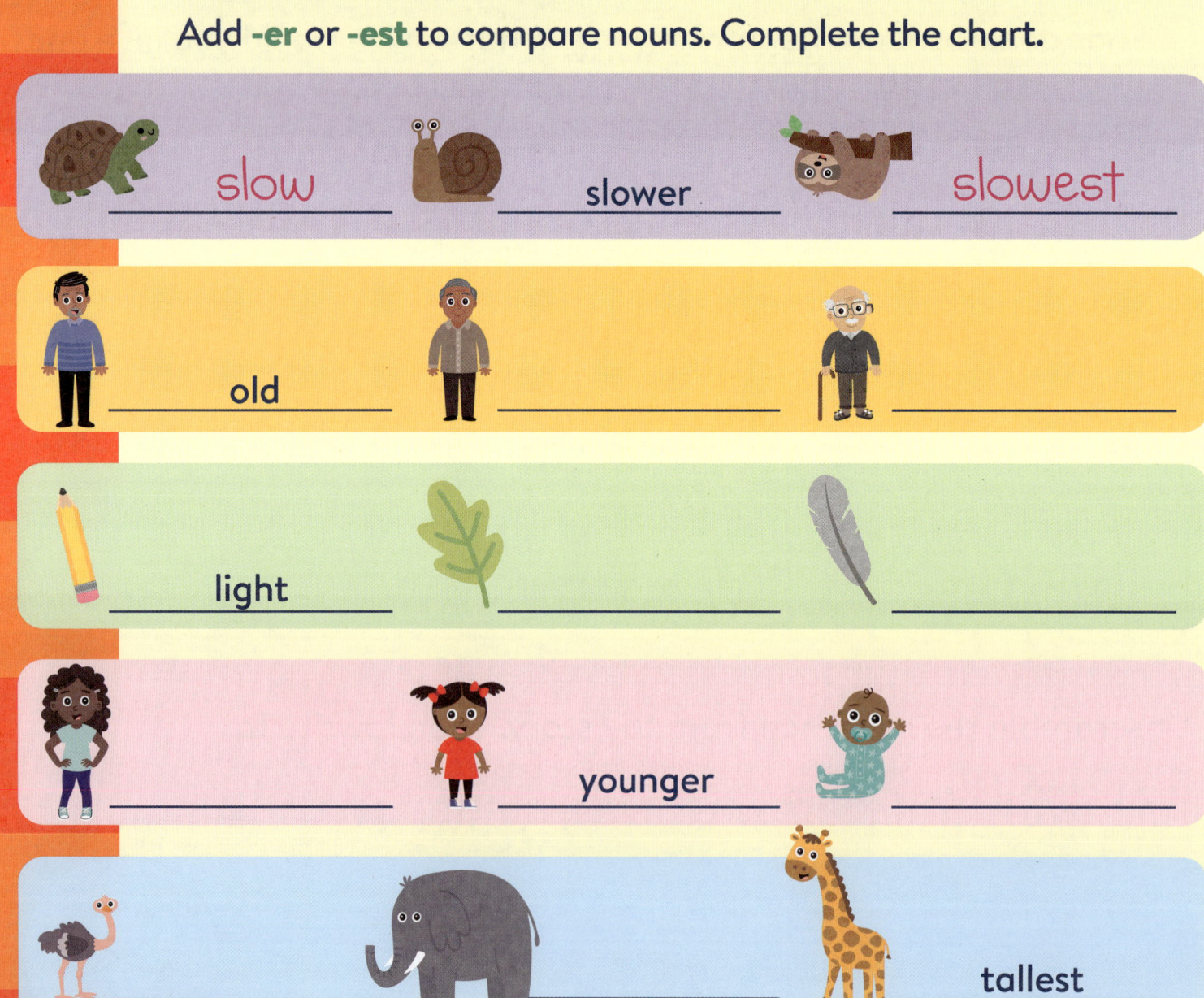

slow   slower   slowest

old

light

younger

tallest

Most of All

Write one word using **-er** or **-est** to replace the blue words in each sentence.

The white cake is the **most plain** cake of them all. ___plainest___

Sam is the **most small** puppy in the litter.

_____

The sofa is **more soft** than the chair.

_____

That flavor is the **most gross** I have ever tried.

_____

A jet would be the **most quick** way to get there.

_____

Nico felt **more calm** already. _____

The cheetah is the **most fast** cat on earth.

_____

Comparing Words

Cat Coins

The letter **c** makes two sounds: **hard c**, like in **cat**, and **soft c**, like in **cent**.

Say the word for each picture. Match the pictures to the box with the word that has the same beginning sound.

cat

cent

celery

crab

cloud

city

cake

camel

Hard and Soft c

Hard and Soft

The **hard c** sound can be in the middle or at the end of a word, or both, like in **picnic**.

The **soft c** sound can be the middle sound of a word, like in **acid**, or at the end, like in **price**.

Circle the word that has the same **c** sound as the picture.

music

face   (act)

pencil

juice   secret

mice

police   cube

picnic

hiccup   rice

cup

uncle   braces

lettuce

ice   corn

Color the clouds showing words that have both the **soft c** and **hard c** sounds.

circle   broccoli   device   arctic

cycle   crack   circus

Hard and Soft c

Personal Titles

An **abbreviation** is a shortened form of a word. Titles like **Dr.** (doctor) and **Mr.** (mister) come before a person's name, like **Dr. Zuck** or **Mr. Chanin**.

Some titles, like **Jr.** (junior) and **Sr.** (senior), come after the name, like **Ken Griffey Sr.** and **Ken Griffey Jr.**

Match the personal title to the abbreviation.

> **Ms.** (say: mizz) is used before a woman's last name. It isn't short for another word. It is just Ms.!

Title	Abbreviation
Doctor	Esq.
Missus	Prof.
Junior	Hon.
Mister	Capt.
Senior	Mr.
Esquire	Sr.
Professor	Mrs.
Captain	Dr.
Honorable	Jr.

Where? How Much?

Streets and measurements are often shortened to abbreviations, like **Ave.** for **Avenue** or **oz.** for **ounce**.

Complete the puzzle with the word that stands for the abbreviation.

Hollywood Blvd   Park Ave

avenue boulevard court foot ounce

pound quart road inch street teaspoon

ACROSS: Measurements
1. in.   9. ft.
5. oz.   10. tsp.
6. qt.   11. lb.

DOWN: Places
2. Ct.   7. Rd.
3. Blvd. 8. Ave.
4. St.

Flower Power

The letters **o** and **u** together make one vowel sound, like in **loud**. The letters **o** and **w** together make one vowel sound, like in **town**.

Look at each picture and say the word out loud. Write **ou** or **ow** to complete each word.

ow

_o_ _w_ l   t __ __ el   br __ __ n

ow

c __ __   cr __ __ n   fl __ __ er

ou

c __ __ ch   cl __ __ d   h __ __ se

Sound It Out

Read the story out loud.
Circle the **ou** or **ow** words
in each sentence.

Then rewrite the words on the lines.

Kitty saw a little (mouse.) _____mouse_____

She jumped down onto the ground.

_____   _____

Kitty made a loud meow.

_____   _____

Mouse made a squeaking sound.

_____   _____

Kitty crouched and prowled.

_____   _____

Mouse ran around and got out of there!

_____   _____   _____

ou and ow

Oyster Maze

The letters **oi** and the letters **oy** make the **/oy/** sound heard in words like **boil** and **toy**.

Say the words in the maze out loud. Connect the words that make the **/oy/** sound to complete the maze.

decoy   vocal   along

ocean   coin   patio   yoga

spoil   onion   cowboy

lion   noise   annoy   joint

noodle   oink   poison

bony   boil   royal   soil

Join the Team

Write **oi** to complete the words in **red** and **oy** to complete the words in **blue**. Then read each word out loud.

b o i l

n _ _ se

t _ _ let

av _ _ d

j _ _ nt

p _ _ nt

b _ _

c _ _

enj _ _

s _ _

oi and oy

Oink Oink

Say the words in the colored boxes aloud. Listen for the **/oy/** sound made by **oi** and **oy**.

Sort the words by writing them in the correct pig pen.

oink   cowboy   soil   enjoy   coil

voice   avoid   noisy   annoy

oi

oink

_____

_____

_____

_____

_____

oy

_____

_____

_____

Enjoy the Toy

Circle the words that make the **/oy/** sound.

A (boy) named Troy jumped for joy when he opened

his present. It was a toy cowboy named Roy. Troy's

sister Joyce made a noise, pointed at the gift, and

said in a loud voice, "Enjoy your toy cowboy, Troy!"

Look at each picture and say the word out loud.

Write **oi** or **oy** in the blanks.

c __ __ n

f __ __ l

__ __ l

p __ __ nt

__ __ ster

oi and oy

Words to Know

Say each letter out loud as you color in **because**, **been**, and **their**. Read each word out loud and write it a few times on the lines below.

because _____

been _____

their _____

Write a word to fill in the blanks.

because   **been**   **their**

Why is there a hole here? The skunks must have

_____ digging all night. The skunks dug

a hole _____ that is how they

make _____ home!

The Case of the Royal Coin

The Royal Coin is a rare, old coin with a picture of a crown on it. Anyone would be thrilled to have this coin because it is one of the rarest coins in the world. When the coin was found missing, everyone knew why it was stolen—the Royal Coin is priceless. The real question was: Who stole it?

There were three suspects, or people who had the chance and reason to steal the coin: Ms. Celine Clifford, Mr. Colton Pierce, and Mrs. Pamela Cartrell. All of them were close to the Royal Coin on the night it was stolen.

The detective continued, "Why is there a secret key, you ask? Well, Ms. Clifford comes from a family that makes safes. Her dad sold the safe to the owner of the coin a long time ago and kept the secret key. When Ms. Clifford had the chance to get close to the Royal Coin, she took it!"

"So it was Ms. Clifford who did it!" said Mr. Pierce.

"Not so fast!" said Detective Hayes. "Ms. Clifford gave the key to Mr. Pierce. As she talked to the guards, Mr. Pierce used the key to take the coin. Ms. Clifford and Mr. Pierce are the sneakiest pair I've ever seen. They both did it!"

The cops took the thieves away and gave the Royal Coin, as well as the secret key, back to their rightful owner. Detective Hayes felt great joy in solving this case.

The coin's owner, Dr. Gilda Geronimo, held a party on the night in question. Dr. Geronimo was one of the richest people in the city. Everyone knew she kept the Royal Coin in a locked safe protected by guards. Dr. Geronimo was the only person with the key.

It would take a clever detective to solve this matter. Detective Hayes, one of the smartest police officers on the force, was put on the case. She brought the suspects together when it was time to tell who stole the Royal Coin and make an arrest.

"It has been one week since the Royal Coin was stolen," said Detective Hayes. "I know someone here has a secret. It is now time for me to tell you who took the Royal Coin."

"Based on my research, I found out that the suspect has the letter c in their first and last name. That means Mrs. Pamela Cartrell did not do it! That leaves Ms. Celine Clifford and Mr. Colton Pierce."

"Then I found an even bigger clue. It turns out that someone else has a secret key to the safe!"

At that moment, everyone gasped. That is, everyone but Ms. Clifford.

Show What You Know

Answer questions about "The Case of the Royal Coin."

What is the Royal Coin?

Who is Detective Hayes?

How do we know that Mrs. Cartrell is not the thief?

List two words from the story with a **hard c** and two words with a **soft c**.

If you could ask a question to one of the characters, who would you ask and what would you ask them?

PLACE STICKER HERE

Sounds the Same to Me!

Homophones are words that sound the same but are spelled differently and have different meanings. **Meat** and **meet** are homophones.

Draw lines to match the homophone pairs.

ate — eight

write — sail

sun — right

see — knight

sale — here

night — son

hear — sea

Oh Dear! A Deer!

Say the words out loud. Match the homophones to the correct pictures.

flower   flour

dear   deer

hair   hare

board   bored

pail   pale

hole   whole

Write a homophone from above next to the matching description.

A powder you use for baking _____flour_____

Animals that grow long antlers _____

Feeling like there is nothing to do _____

Something colorful that grows in soil _____

Animal that looks like a rabbit _____

A flat piece of wood _____

It grows on your head _____

Prefix Planting

The prefix **re-** means "again." **Rewash** means to "wash again." The prefix **non-** means "not." **Nonstop** means "not stopping."

Write each prefix with a base word from a petal to create new words. Write the new words in the matching column.

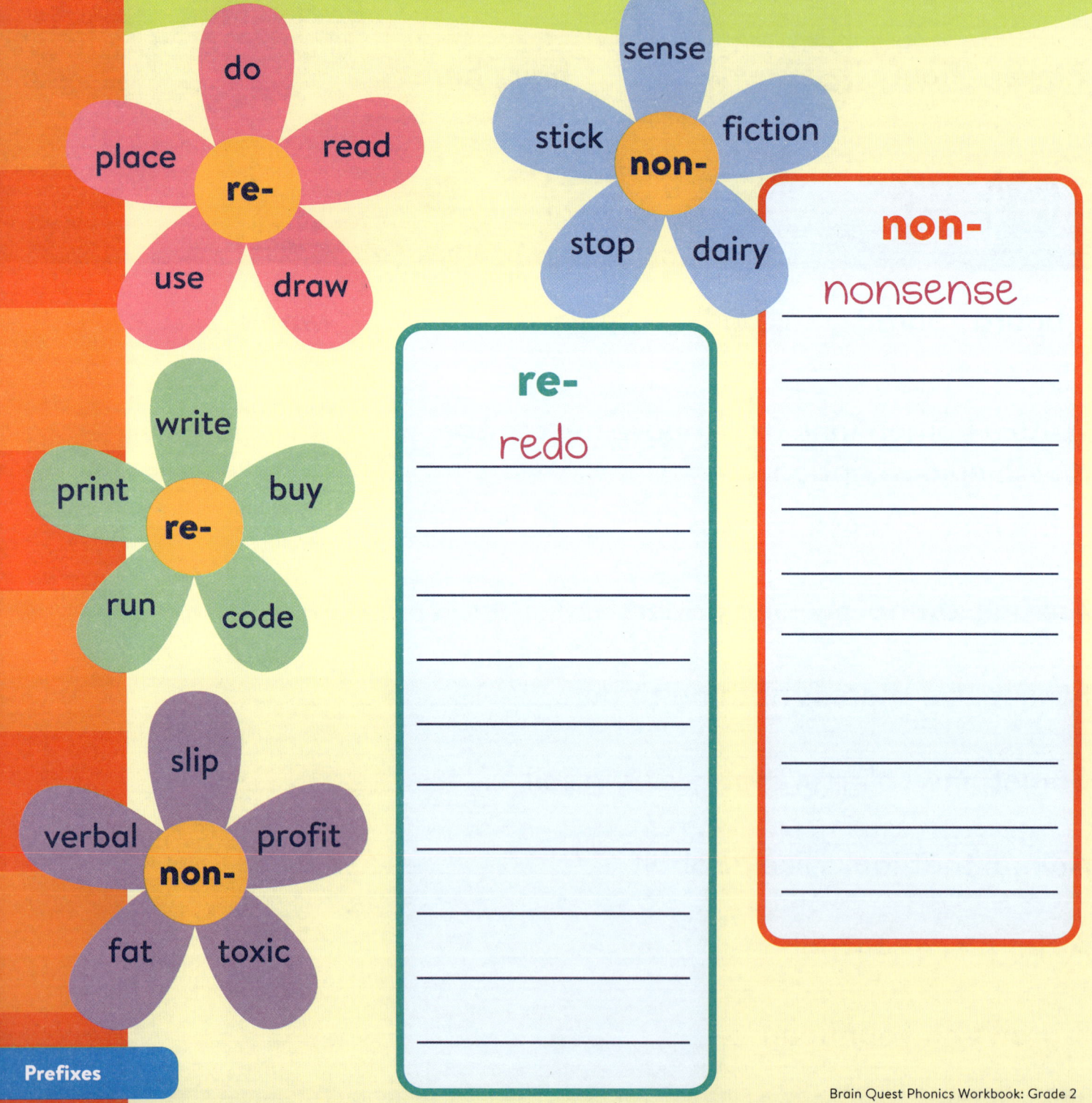

re-

do

place • read

re-

use • draw

write

print • buy

re-

run • code

slip

verbal • profit

non-

fat • toxic

sense

stick • fiction

non-

stop • dairy

re-
redo
_____
_____
_____
_____
_____
_____
_____
_____

non-
nonsense
_____
_____
_____
_____
_____
_____
_____

Shopping for Prefixes

Fill in the missing word in each sentence.

replaced   rethink   rewrite   nondairy   nonstick

We need a _____ pan so the cakes will come out easily.

I can't drink cow's milk. Is there _____ milk here?

I'm sorry, there isn't. I will _____ my orders!

I think this price tag needs to be _____ .

I will _____ the price tag right now!

Brain Quest Phonics Workbook: Grade 2

Prefixes

An Invisible Painter

The suffixes **-er** and **-or** both mean "a person who." A person who **bakes** is a **baker**. A person who **edits** is an **editor**.

Add the suffix **-er** or **-or** to make the name of a job.

-er

teach <u>e r</u>

work __ __

paint __ __

sing __ __

-or

act <u>o r</u>

sail __ __

invent __ __

visit __ __

The suffix **-able** means "able to." Add **-able** to the words below to make new words. Write the new words.

verb + able =

buy __buyable__

treat _____

fold _____

accept _____

break _____

fix _____

BRAIN BOX

The suffix **-ible** is usually added to a word part: **vis + ible = visible**. The suffix **-able** is usually added to a complete word: **fix + able = fixable**.

Suffixes

Suffix Sort

The suffixes **-sion** and **-tion** change a verb to a noun. These suffixes mean *the act of*. **Election** means "the act of electing someone."

Say the words in the colored boxes aloud. Sort the words by suffix into the correct group.

education   vision   decision   addition

expression   infection   action   confusion

erosion   option

Write the words on the lines.

-sion

_____

_____   _____

_____   _____

-tion

_____

_____   _____

_____   _____

BRAIN BOX

The suffixes **-sion** and **-tion** are usually pronounced with a **/sh/** sound, like in **expression**, or a **/zh/** sound, like in **conclusion**. When the letter **s** comes before **-tion**, the word has a **/ch/** sound, like in **digestion**.

Pick a Prefix

Prefix	Meaning	Example
un-	not	unwell
re-	again	redo
dis-	opposite of	disagree
pre-	before	preheat

Circle the missing word and write it in the blank.

Mr. Aronson was ____unhappy____ with his class.

(unhappy)   nonhappy   prehappy

They were _____ to behave!

disable   preable   unable

The class was _____ every rule.

misobeying   preobeying   disobeying

He just wanted to teach them to _____

questions before a test!   disread   preread   unread

So Many Suffixes

Underline the suffix for each word in the example column.

Suffix	Meaning	Example
-ly	in a way that is	slow<u>ly</u>
-er	more	funnier
-est	most	fastest
-er/-or	a person who	player

Circle the missing word and write it in the blank.

I love my Aunt Flor. She is the _____ person in the world. nicer   nicor   nicest

She is _____ than most people I know. silliest   sillier   sillyly

She is a _____ for a second grade class.

teachor   teacher   teachest

Aunt Flor runs very _____.
I can't beat her in a race!
quicky   quickest   quickly

Say It Twice!

Homographs are words that have the same spelling but sound different and have different meanings. For example, **wind**, which rhymes with *pinned*, is a noun that means "moving air." **Wind**, which rhymes with *mind*, is a verb that means "to twist something."

Say the name of each picture and write the homograph shown. Then draw a line connecting the homograph pairs.

bow	tear	record	bass

Write one sentence with two homographs in it. For example: The **wind** knocked over my watch and I had to **wind** it again to show the correct time.

_____

More Homographs

Each word in the colored boxes can be said two ways.
Read each sentence and write the missing word.
Then read the sentence out loud to make sure you are
saying the right homograph!

`lead`   `live`   `minute`   `close`

It's time to _____ the book and go to sleep.

Felix will _____ his soccer team to victory!

I _____ next to a beautiful garden.

Zoe always takes a _____ to double-check
her work before turning it in.

Clyde loves to watch _____ soccer games in
a stadium.

Ms. Amy used a microscope to show us a
_____ cell.

The Romans transported water to their cities using
_____ pipes.

It's fun to live _____ to school. I can walk
there in three minutes!

> **Minute** (pronounced my-newt) also means "very small."

Homographs

Put It Together

A **contraction** is a type of word that combines two or more words in a shortened form. For example, **they're** is a contraction for **they are.** Contractions use these punctuation marks ' called **apostrophes.**

I'm = I am

she's = she is

you're = you are

they'll = they will

he's = he is

we'll = we will

Circle the correct contraction to fill in the blank. Then write it on the line.

Heather said she would help me at 5:00 p.m. and _____she's_____ never late.   you're   (she's)

_____ hoping that we can bake cookies together.   I'm   They'll

BRAIN BOX

The **apostrophe** takes the place of the letters that drop out when words are written as contractions.

If Heather helps with the cookies, _____ taste delicious.   he's   they'll

_____ have fun together. We always do!   We'll   You're

Contraction Action

can't = cannot	won't = will not
don't = do not	isn't = is not

Write the word or words that make up each contraction.

don't _____do not_____   isn't _____

can't _____   won't _____

Read each sentence. Circle the word or words that could be rewritten with a contraction. Write the contraction on the line.

I (cannot) wait for the big day! _____can't_____

I do not want to spoil the surprise for my little brother.

_____

He is not going to believe it. _____

We are taking him on a trip to New York City that he will not forget. _____

Words to Know

Say each letter out loud as you color in **could**, **only**, and **right**. Read each word out loud and write it a few times on the lines below.

could _____

only _____

right _____

Write a word to fill in the blanks.

| could | only | right |

There are _____ three days until we

fly to California! I can't wait to sit in the sun

_____ under a palm tree. I _____

spend every day like that. Maybe I will!

High-Frequency Words

Pirate Pete's Flea Market

We Accept Silver, Gold, And Jewels Only

Pirate Pete knows how to sell. Watch what happens when a shopper walks in.

"Ahoy! Welcome to Pirate Pete's Flea Market," said Pirate Pete. "Do you like feeling the wind in your hair as you sail the high seas? We have any item a sailor could want!"

Pirate Pete kept talking. "This rope makes the strongest knots! It is flexible and bendable."

"Well, I—" started the shopper.

"Eye? You're looking for an eye patch? Aye, I've got that! You will be able to see the blue sea like never before."

1

Pirate Pete smiled his biggest smile yet. "We take silver coins, gold coins, and jewels only. No apps."

The shopper grinned and said, "That's too bad. I don't have cash. Bye-bye!"

Pirate Pete gritted his teeth and yelled, "Thanks for stopping by!"

4

"I was wondering if you have time—" the shopper mumbled.

"Yes, sir, we have the time! We have many wind-up clocks and other timekeepers!"

The shopper looked pale. Pirate Pete did not pause.

"Blimey! You don't look so good, matey. Want to buy a pail? We have the biggest selection of sizes and colors on the high seas."

The shopper tried again. "Sorry, I'm not looking to buy—"

"Maybe you're looking for a sale! We're having a sail sale right now! We have the brightest sails too. Plus, they are all nonstick. How many sails for your ship? Would two do?"

"But I'm not a—" the shopper said.

But Pirate Pete would not stop. "Would you like something thicker? Thinner? Smaller? Wider?"

"OK!" shouted the shopper. "I'll buy anything! Just tell me how to find Main Street!"

Show What You Know

Answer questions about "Pirate Pete's Flea Market."

What are some things for sale at Pirate Pete's Flea Market?

Why is Pirate Pete good at selling?

List three sets of words from the story that sound the same but have different spellings and meanings.

High-Frequency Words

Point to each high-frequency word as you read it aloud.

around   awake   because   been

before   both   buy   could

don't   enough   first

found   it's   once   only

read   right   says   should

something   their   these

through   upon   very

which   work

would   your

BRAIN BOX

These are words you learned in this book. If you don't know a word yet, look for sounds you do know in the word. Remember some of the spelling patterns are tricky, so you may need to try a few times!

Answer Key

Pages 6–7

Pages 8–9

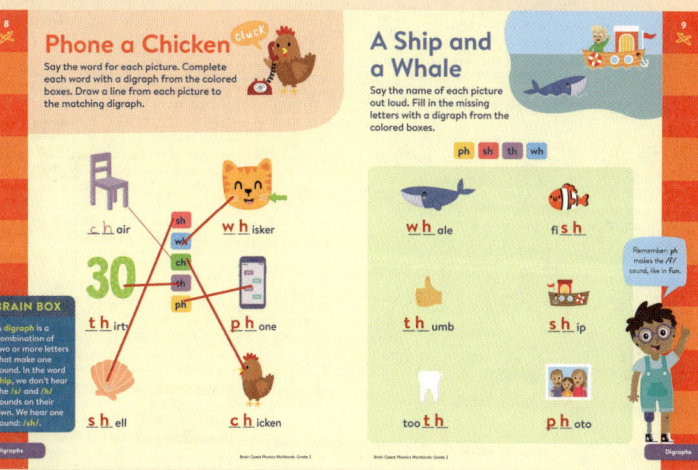

Pages 10–11

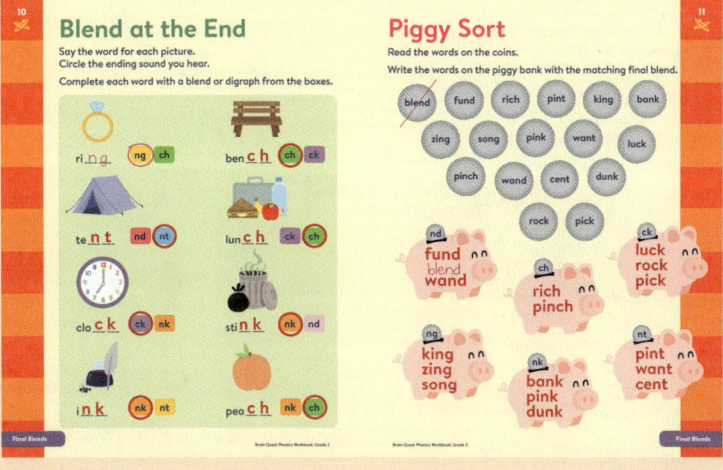

Page 12

Page 15

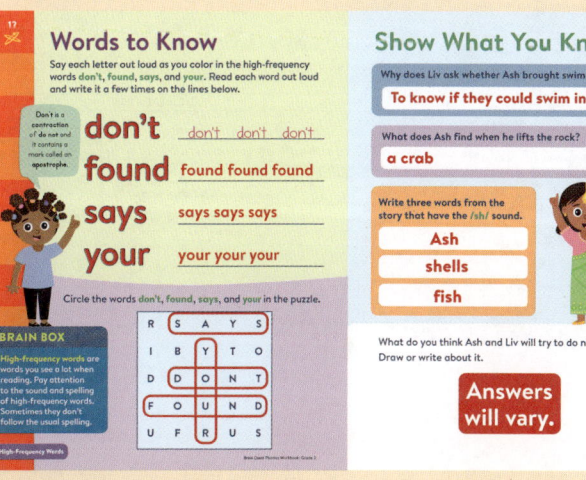

Pages 16–17

Pages 18–19

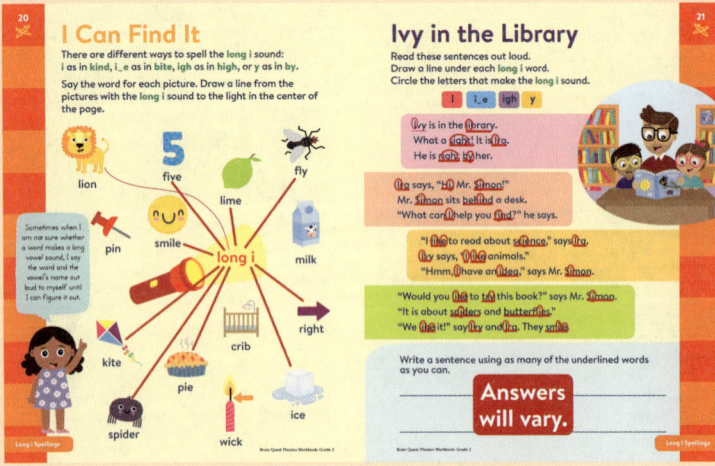

I Can Find It

There are different ways to spell the long i sound: i as in kind, i_e as in bite, igh as in high, or y as in by.

Say the word for each picture. Draw a line from the pictures with the long i sound to the light in the center of the page.

Sometimes when I am not sure whether a word makes a long vowel sound, I say the word and the vowel's name out loud to myself until I can figure it out.

lion · five · fly · lime · smile · milk · pin · long i · right · crib · kite · pie · ice · spider · wick

Ivy in the Library

Read these sentences out loud. Draw a line under each long i word. Circle the letters that make the long i sound.

i · i_e · igh · y

Ivy is in the library. What a ride! It is Ivy. He is right by her.

Ivy says, "Hi Mr. Simon." Mr. Simon sits behind a desk. "What can I help you find?" he says.

"I like to read about science," says Ivy. Ivy says, "I like animals." "Hmm, I have an idea," says Mr. Simon.

"Would you like to try this book?" says Mr. Simon. "It is about spiders and butterflies." "We like it!" say Ivy and Ira. They smile.

Write a sentence using as many of the underlined words as you can.

Answers will vary.

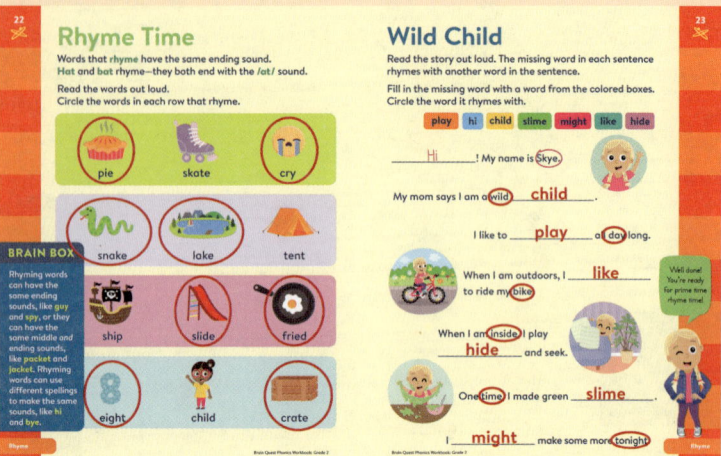

Rhyme Time

Words that rhyme have the same ending sound. Hat and bat rhyme—they both end with the /at/ sound.

Read the words out loud. Circle the words in each row that rhyme.

pie · skate · cry
snake · lake · tent
ship · slide · fried
eight · child · crate

BRAIN BOX

Rhyming words can have the same ending sounds, like guy and say, or they can have the same middle and ending sounds, like packet and jacket. Rhyming words can use different spellings to make the same sounds, like hi and bye.

Wild Child

Read the story out loud. The missing word in each sentence rhymes with another word in the sentence.

Fill in the missing word with a word from the colored boxes. Circle the word it rhymes with.

play · hi · child · slime · might · like · hide

___Hi___ ! My name is Skye.

My mom says I am a wild ___child___ .

I like to ___play___ at day long.

When I am outdoors, I ___like___ to ride my bike.

Well done! You're ready for prime time rhyme time!

When I am inside I play ___hide___ and seek.

One time I made green ___slime___ .

I ___might___ make some more tonight.

Oh, Hello!

There are different ways to spell the long o sound: o as in go, o_e as in hole, oa as in toad, ow as in low, and oe as in doe.

Say the word for each picture. Complete the long o words using the letters in the colored boxes.

o · oa · oe · ow · a_e

c_oa_t · g_o_ld · pill_ow_
r_o_se · s_oa_p · b_ow_l
n_o_se · b_oa_t · b_ow_
yell_ow_ · t_oe_ · r_o_se

Let's Go!

Read the article. Circle the words with the long o sound. Then write the long o words on the correct vowel card.

LOCAL GOAL

Coach throws the ball to a player on the field. Hugo runs and passes the ball to Moe. Moe shoots the ball close to the goal. The whole team shouts, "Let's go!" Then Joan kicks it in with her toe. Goal!

oa like boat
coach
goal
Joan

ow like snow
throws

o_e like home
close
whole

oe like doe
Moe
toe

o like open
go
Hugo

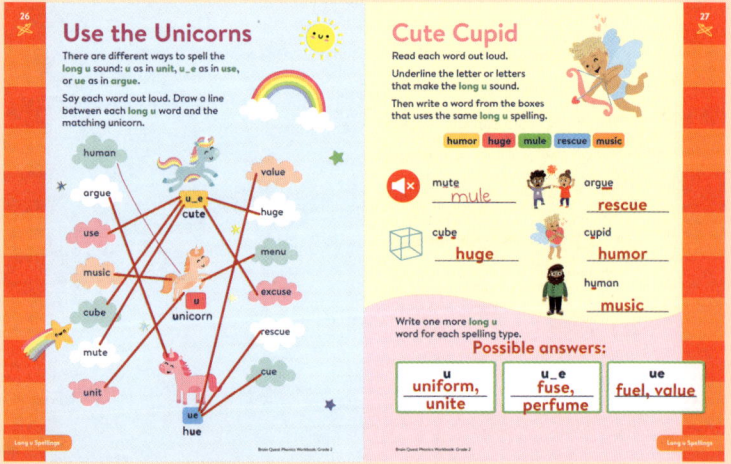

Use the Unicorns

There are different ways to spell the long u sound: u as in unit, u_e as in use, or ue as in argue.

Say each word out loud. Draw a line between each long u word and the matching unicorn.

human · argue · use · music · cube · mute · unit · cute · u_e · unicorn · u · ue · hue · value · huge · menu · excuse · rescue · cue

Cute Cupid

Read each word out loud. Underline the letter or letters that make the long u sound.

Then write a word from the boxes that uses the same long u spelling.

humor · huge · mule · rescue · music

mute — ___mule___   argue — ___rescue___
cube — ___huge___   cupid — ___humor___
human — ___music___

Write one more long u word for each spelling type.

Possible answers:

u	u_e	ue
uniform, unite	fuse, perfume	fuel, value

Field Bunny

There are different ways to spell the long e sound: e as in be, ea as in eat, ee as in see, ey as in key, e_e as in eve, ie as in chief, i as in ski, and y as in copy.

Circle the letter or letters that make the long e sound in each word.

Match the long e words that have the same long e spelling.

beach · bee · cookie · dream · ski · field · Hero · baby · turkey · taxi · feet · equal · bunny · monkey

Queen E

Read each word out loud. Circle the part of each word that makes the long e sound.

e · ea · ee · ey · ie

queen · meow · seal · puppy · key · movie · teeth · candy · beach

Great job with long e sound!

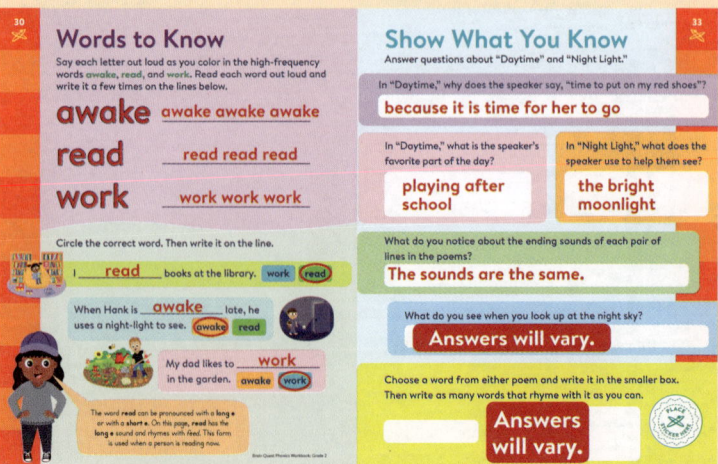

Words to Know

Say each letter out loud as you color in the high-frequency words awake, read, and work. Read each word out loud and write it a few times on the lines below.

awake — awake awake awake

read — read read read

work — work work work

Circle the correct word. Then write it on the line.

I ___read___ books at the library. work / read

When Hank is ___awake___ late, he uses a night-light to see. awake / read

My dad likes to ___work___ in the garden. awake / work

The word read can be pronounced with a long e or with a short e. On this page, read has the long e sound and rhymes with feed. This form is used when a person is reading now.

Show What You Know

Answer questions about "Daytime" and "Night Light."

In "Daytime," why does the speaker say, "time to put on my red shoes"?
because it is time for her to go

In "Daytime," what is the speaker's favorite part of the day?
playing after school

In "Night Light," what does the speaker use to help them see?
the bright moonlight

What do you notice about the ending sounds of each pair of lines in the poems?
The sounds are the same.

What do you see when you look up at the night sky?
Answers will vary.

Choose a word from either poem and write it in the smaller box. Then write as many words that rhyme with it as you can.

Answers will vary.

Pages 34–35

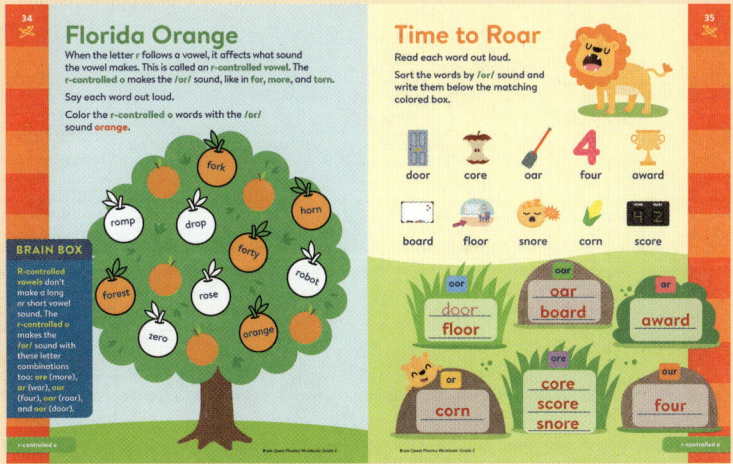

Pages 36–37

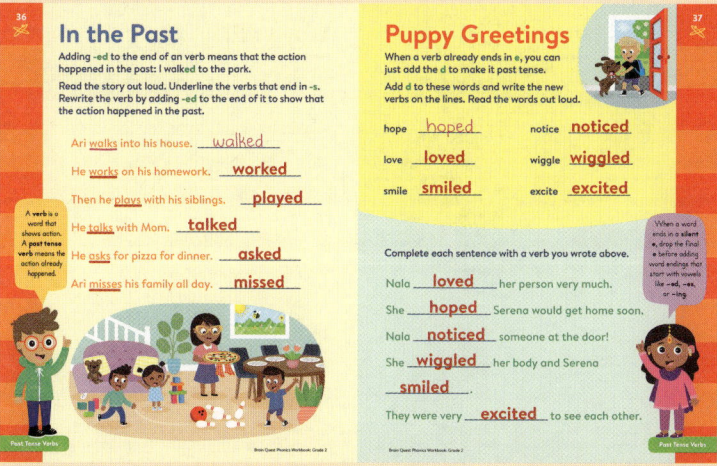

Pages 38–39

Pages 40–41

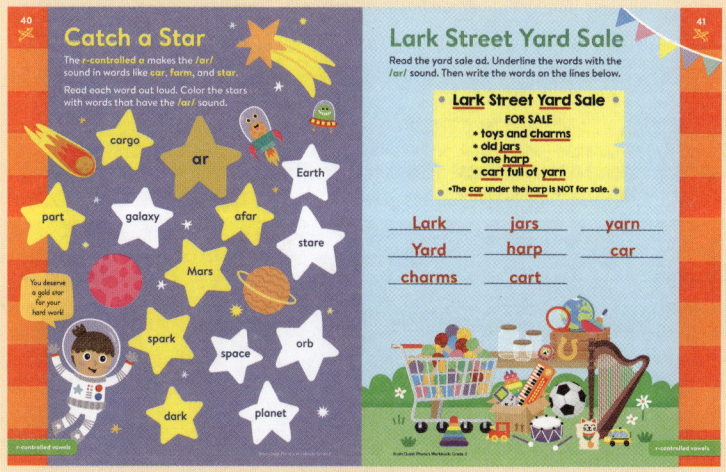

Pages 42–43

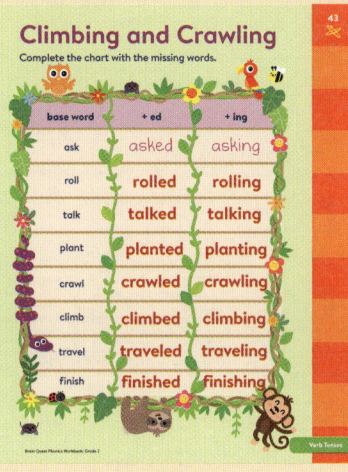

Page 44   Page 47

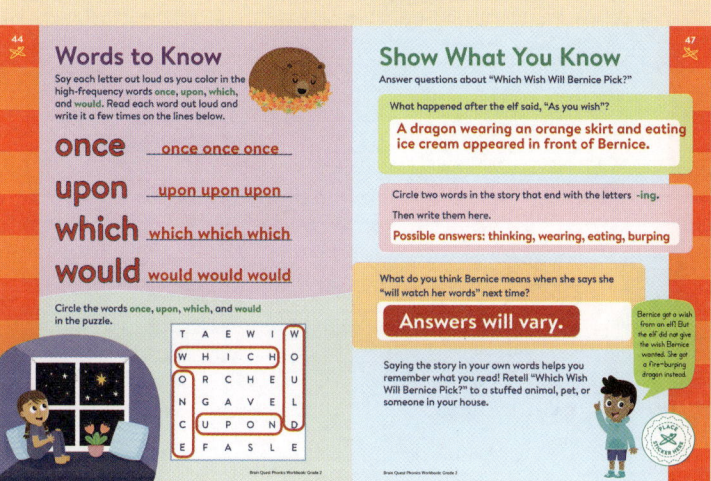

Pages 48–49

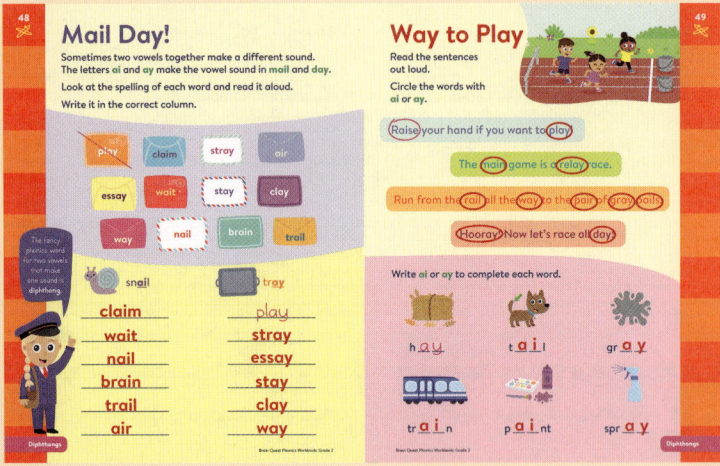

Mail Day!

Sometimes two vowels together make a different sound. The letters ai and ay make the vowel sound in mail and day.

Look at the spelling of each word and read it aloud. Write it in the correct column.

play, claim, stray, air, essay, wait, stay, clay, way, nail, brain, trail

snail · tray

claim	play
wait	stray
nail	essay
brain	stay
trail	clay
air	way

Way to Play

Read the sentences out loud. Circle the words with ai or ay.

Raise your hand if you want to play.

The main game is a relay race.

Run from the trail all the way to the pair of gray rails.

Hooray! Now let's race all day!

Write ai or ay to complete each word.

h a y · t ai l · gr ay

tr ai n · p ai nt · spr ay

Pages 50–51

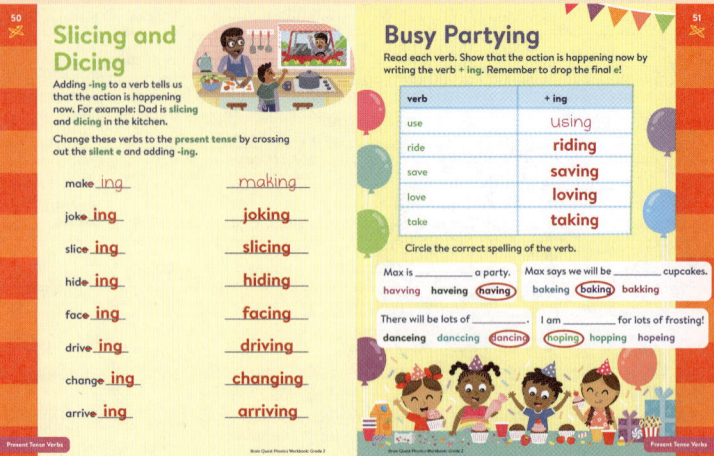

Slicing and Dicing

Adding -ing to a verb tells us that the action is happening now. For example: Dad is slicing and dicing in the kitchen.

Change these verbs to the present tense by crossing out the silent e and adding -ing.

make ing — making
joke ing — joking
slice ing — slicing
hide ing — hiding
face ing — facing
drive ing — driving
change ing — changing
arrive ing — arriving

Busy Partying

Read each verb. Show that the action is happening now by writing the verb + ing. Remember to drop the final e!

verb	+ ing
use	using
ride	riding
save	saving
love	loving
take	taking

Circle the correct spelling of the verb.

Max is _____ a party. | Max says we will be _____ cupcakes.
havving heaving (having) | bakeing (baking) bakking

There will be lots of _____ | I am _____ for lots of frosting!
danceing dancceing (dancing) | (hoping) hopping hopeing

Pages 52–53

Splish-Splash

Screw, splash, spring, and strong begin with three-letter blends.

To read a word beginning with a three-letter blend, say the sound each letter makes and then say the sounds together to blend them.

Read the words out loud. Write each word on the card with the matching blend.

strong, spray, spring, splat, stroll, split, string, scroll, sprint, splash, screen, screw

str	spl
strong	splash
string	split
stroll	splat

scr	spr
screen	spray
screw	spring
scroll	sprint

Strawberry Blend

Pick a blend from the blender to complete the words below.

scr, spl, spr, str

Words with three-letter blends can be tricky to say. They have three consonants with no vowels between them! Practice saying each letter sound until you can blend them smoothly.

s t r ipe · s c r atch · s p r ay

s t r eet · s t r aw · s p l at

Pages 54–55

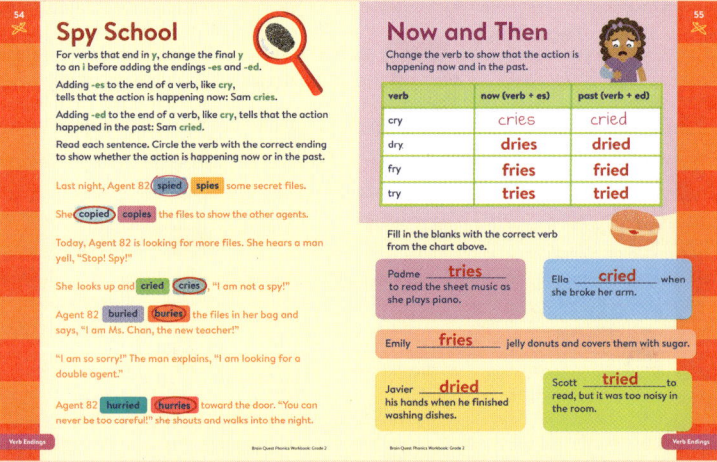

Spy School

For verbs that end in y, change the final y to an i before adding the endings -es and -ed.

Adding -es to the end of a verb, like cry, tells that the action is happening now: Sam cries.

Adding -ed to the end of a verb, like cry, tells that the action happened in the past: Sam cried.

Read each sentence. Circle the verb with the correct ending to show whether the action is happening now or in the past.

Last night, Agent 82 spied / (spies) some secret files.

She (copied) / copies the files to show the other agents.

Today, Agent 82 is looking for more files. She hears a man yell, "Stop! Spy!"

She looks up and (cried) / cries, "I am not a spy!"

Agent 82 buried / (buries) the files in her bag and says, "I am Ms. Chan, the new teacher!"

"I am so sorry!" The man explains, "I am looking for a double agent."

Agent 82 hurried / (hurries) toward the door. "You can never be too careful!" she shouts and walks into the night.

Now and Then

Change the verb to show that the action is happening now and in the past.

verb	now (verb + es)	past (verb + ed)
cry	cries	cried
dry	dries	dried
fry	fries	fried
try	tries	tried

Fill in the blanks with the correct verb from the chart above.

Padme **tries** to read the sheet music as she plays piano.

Ella **cried** when she broke her arm.

Emily **fries** jelly donuts and covers them with sugar.

Javier **dried** his hands when he finished washing dishes.

Scott **tried** to read, but it was too noisy in the room.

Pages 56–57

So Many Things

Write a word from the colored boxes under each picture.

Add s to the end of the word if the picture shows more than one of each item.

bike, friend, scooter, dog, grape, swing

grapes, scooters, bike, swing, friends, dogs

A noun is a person, place, or thing. A plural noun means there is more than one, usually ending in s.

Kitchen Counting

If a noun ends in s, x, z, ch, or sh, add -es to make it plural.

Write the correct word below the object. Add a final -s or -es if there is more than one.

apple, glass, pot, dish, box, table

boxes, pot, apples, glasses, table, dishes

Page 58

Words to Know

Say each letter out loud as you color in the high-frequency words should, something, and very. Read each word out loud and write it a few times on the lines below.

should should should should

something something something something

very very very very

Circle the correct word. Then write it on the line.

Drinking hot cocoa **should** help warm you up on a cold day. very (should)

I want to teach my baby sister to say **something** funny. (something) very

Bananas start out **very** green and then turn yellow as they ripen. should (very)

Page 61

Show What You Know

Answer questions about "Fun Facts About Spruce Trees."

Write two words that tell how spruce trees look.
Possible answers: large, green, tall, straight

What can be made from spruce wood?
Possible answers: timber, instruments, toys

What can be made from spruce resin?
Possible answers: gum, drinks, tar

Draw a spruce tree.

Write a verb from the text that ends in the letters -ing.
Possible answers: saying, building, making

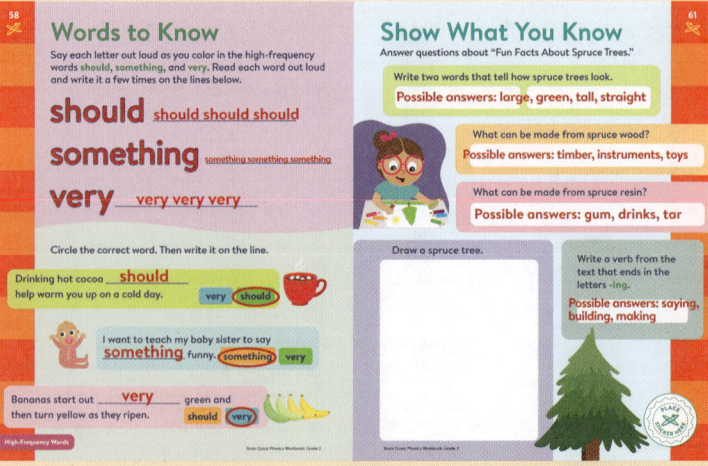

Pages 62–63

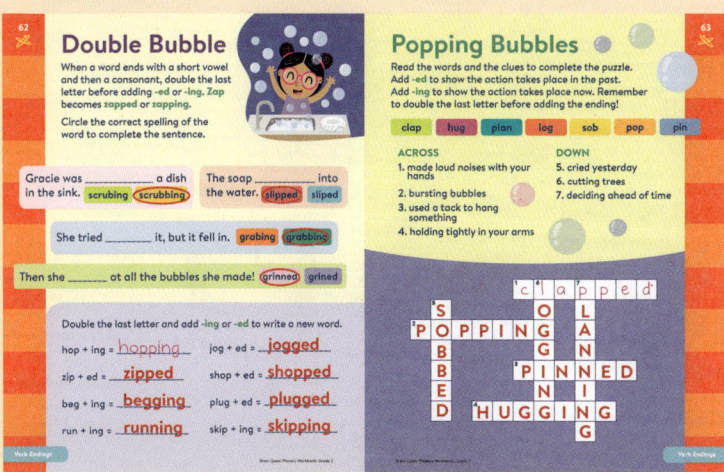

Pages 64–65

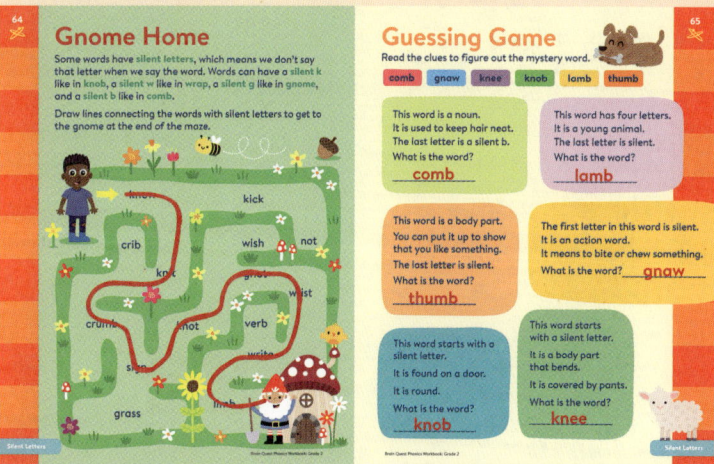

Pages 66–67

Pages 68–69

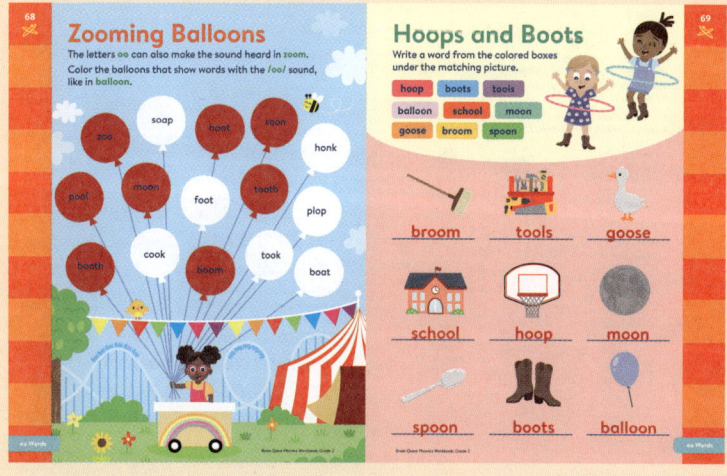

Pages 70–71

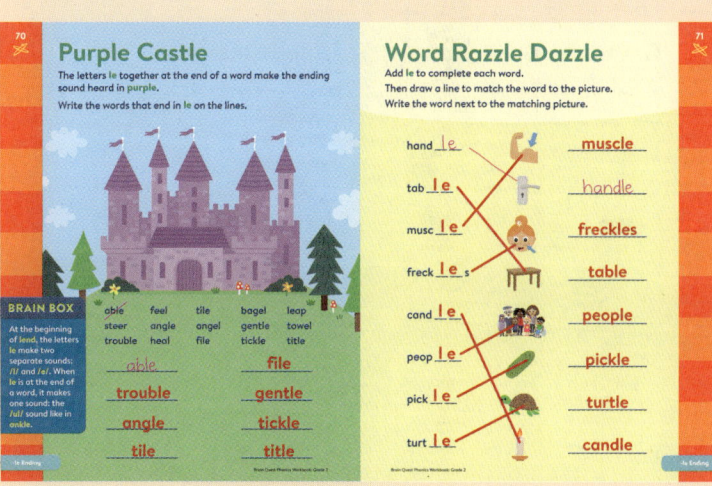

Pages 72–73

Page 74

Words to Know
Say each letter out loud as you color in **before**, **first**, and **these**. Read each word out loud and write it a few times on the lines below.

before _before before before_

first _first first first_

these _these these these_

Read the clues and complete the puzzle with the words **before**, **first**, and **these**.

ACROSS
1. _____, second, third
2. plural form of *this*

DOWN
3. _____ and after

Crossword answers:
'F I R S T
'T H E S E
B
F
O
R
E

Page 77

Show What You Know
Answer questions about "Making Sparkle Cookies."

What is the first step to make sparkle cookies?
Put the cookies on the tray.

What step comes after stirring the icing?
Spreading the icing on top of the cookies

Why should you let the cookies sit?
It helps the sprinkles stick.

Write two compound words from the text here.
rainbow | teaspoons

If you could add any topping to cookies, what would you add?
Answers will vary.

Pages 78–79

Play Time
When f, l, s, or z is at the end of a word, the letter is sometimes doubled to become ff, ll, ss, or zz. You can find this at the end of words like **puff**, **grill**, **hiss**, and **buzz**.

Write the word from the box that matches each picture.

ball | chess | doll | dress
fluff | shell | fizz

shell
fizz
ball
chess
dress
doll
fluff

Double Up
Write a double final consonant from the colored boxes to make a word.

ff | ll | ss | zz

be_ll_
cli_ff_
gra_ss_
tro_ll_
ja_zz_
wa_ll_
ki_ss_
o_ff_

Pages 80–81

The Juggling Rabbit
Many words have these double consonants in the middle: bb, dd, gg, mm, nn, pp, or tt.

The double consonants tell readers that the beginning of the word has a short vowel sound.

Circle the missing letters that complete the word. Then write the letters in the blanks and read the word out loud.

ra_bb_it
hi_pp_o
ha_mm_ock
ju_gg_le
la_dd_er
ki_tt_en
pe_nn_y

Apple Sort
Say each word in the colored boxes. Sort the words by double consonants on the cards below.

ribbon | summer | puppy | minnow | tennis
attic | winner | mammal | happy | wedding
muddy | baggy | pebble | comma | dribble
jiggle | attend | written | puppet

bb	dd	gg	mm
ribbon	wedding	baggy	summer
pebble	muddy	jiggle	mammal
dribble			comma

nn	pp	tt
winner	puppy	attic
minnow	happy	attend
tennis	puppet	written

Pages 82–83

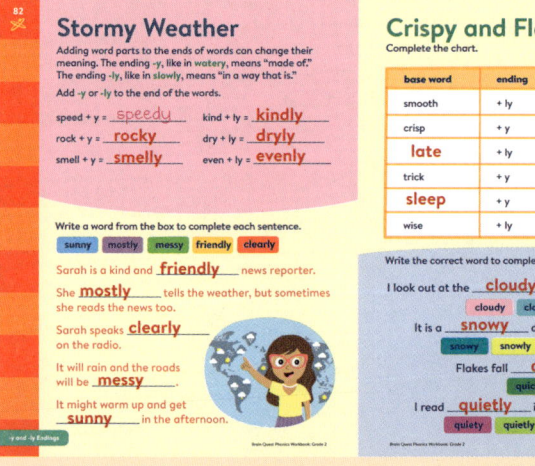

Stormy Weather
Adding word parts to the ends of words can change their meaning. The ending -y, like in **watery**, means "made of." The ending -ly, like in **slowly**, means "in a way that is."

Add -y or -ly to the end of the words.

speed + y = _speedy_
rock + y = _rocky_
smell + y = _smelly_
kind + ly = _kindly_
dry + ly = _dryly_
even + ly = _evenly_

Write a word from the box to complete each sentence.
sunny | mostly | messy | friendly | clearly

Sarah is a kind and _friendly_ news reporter.
She _mostly_ tells the weather, but sometimes she reads the news too.
Sarah speaks _clearly_ on the radio.
It will rain and the roads will be _messy_.
It might warm up and get _sunny_ in the afternoon.

Crispy and Flaky
Complete the chart.

base word	ending	new word
smooth	+ ly	smoothly
crisp	+ y	crispy
late	+ ly	lately
trick	+ y	tricky
sleep	+ y	sleepy
wise	+ ly	wisely

Write the correct word to complete each sentence.

I look out at the _cloudy_ sky. (cloudy / cloudly)
It is a _snowy_ day today. (snowy / snowly)
Flakes fall _quickly_. (quicky / quickly)
I read _quietly_ in my room. (quiety / quietly)

Pages 84–85

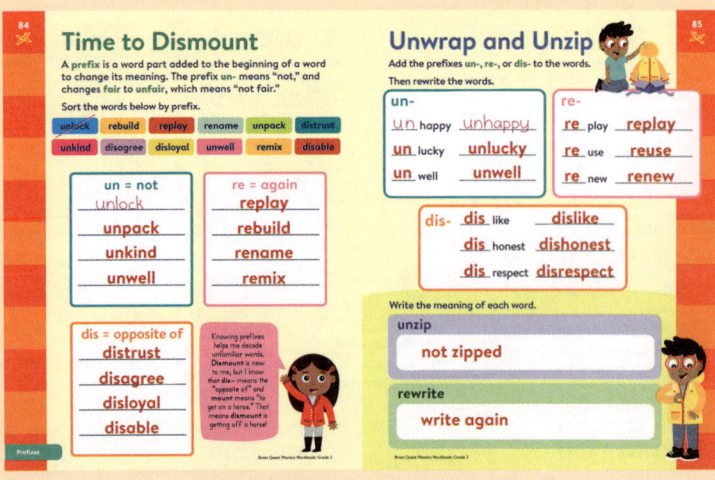

Time to Dismount
A **prefix** is a word part added to the beginning of a word to change its meaning. The prefix **un-** means "not," and changes **fair** to **unfair**, which means "not fair."

Sort the words below by prefix.
unlock | rebuild | replay | rename | unpack | distrust
unkind | disagree | disloyal | unwell | remix | disable

un = not	re = again
unlock	replay
unpack	rebuild
unkind	rename
unwell	remix

dis = opposite of
distrust
disagree
disloyal
disable

Unwrap and Unzip
Add the prefixes un-, re-, or dis- to the words. Then rewrite the words.

un- _happy_ = _unhappy_
un _lucky_ = _unlucky_
un _well_ = _unwell_

re- _play_ = _replay_
re _use_ = _reuse_
re _new_ = _renew_

dis- _like_ = _dislike_
dis _honest_ = _dishonest_
dis _respect_ = _disrespect_

Write the meaning of each word.
unzip — not zipped
rewrite — write again

Pages 86–87

Get to the Gym!
The letter g makes two sounds: hard g, like in **get** or **frog**, and soft g, like in **gym** or **age**.
Sort the words onto the hard g or soft g card.

cage | game | glue | magic | log | giraffe | germ | goat | grapes | gem | dragon

hard g
game, glue, log, goat, grapes, dragon

soft g
cage, magic, giraffe, germ, gem

Good Oranges
Circle the word with the same g sound as the picture.

orange — pig / (page)
frog — (hug) / wedge
sponge — (stage) / plug
mug — (flag) / veggie
eagle — (bug) / urge
cage — dig / (magic)
dog — age / (bag)
judge — (range) / ping
bridge — (angel) / beg
dragon — edge / (grow)

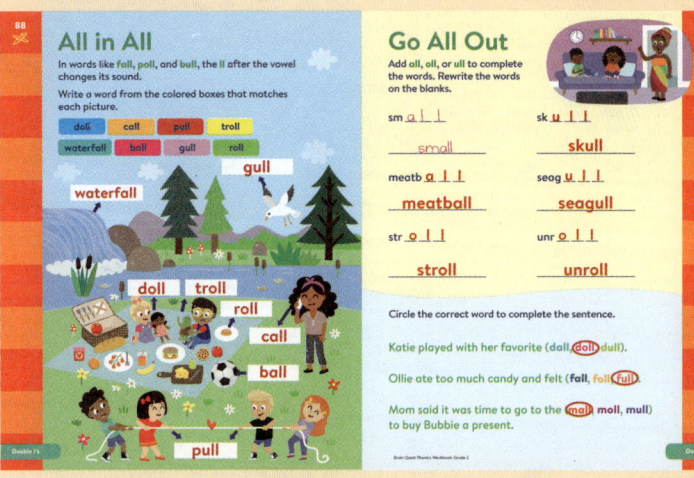

All in All

In words like **fall**, **poll**, and **bull**, the **ll** after the vowel changes its sound.

Write a word from the colored boxes that matches each picture.

doll | call | pull | troll
waterfall | ball | gull | roll

gull

waterfall

doll | troll

roll

call

ball

pull

Go All Out

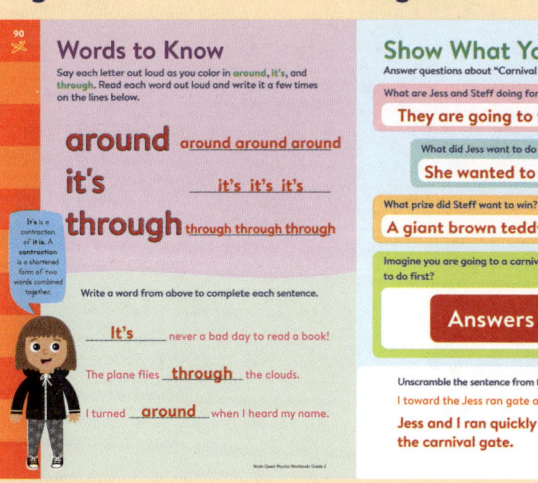

Add **all**, **oll**, or **ull** to complete the words. Rewrite the words on the blanks.

sm a l l
small

meatb a l l
meatball

str o l l
stroll

sk u l l
skull

seag u l l
seagull

unr o l l
unroll

Circle the correct word to complete the sentence.

Katie played with her favorite (dall, **doll**, dull).

Ollie ate too much candy and felt (fall, foll, **full**).

Mom said it was time to go to the (**mall**, moll, mull) to buy Bubbie a present.

Words to Know

Say each letter out loud as you color in **around**, **it's**, and **through**. Read each word out loud and write it a few times on the lines below.

around — around around around

it's — it's it's it's

through — through through through

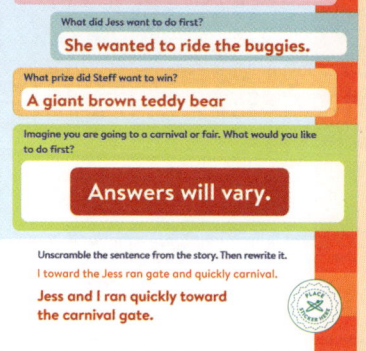

It is a contraction of it is. A contraction is a shortened form of two words combined together.

Write a word from above to complete each sentence.

It's never a bad day to read a book!

The plane flies through the clouds.

I turned around when I heard my name.

Show What You Know

Answer questions about "Carnival Buzz."

What are Jess and Steff doing for the day?
They are going to the carnival.

What did Jess want to do first?
She wanted to ride the buggies.

What prize did Steff want to win?
A giant brown teddy bear

Imagine you are going to a carnival or fair. What would you like to do first?
Answers will vary.

Unscramble the sentence from the story. Then rewrite it.
I toward the Jess ran gate and quickly carnival.
Jess and I ran quickly toward the carnival gate.

Plural Practice

Adding **s** or **es** to the end of a noun makes many words plural. **Irregular plurals** are words that do not follow this rule.

Write the irregular plural of the singular word.

people | men | children | women

Singular: One	Plural: More Than One
man	men
woman	women
child	children
person	people

BRAIN BOX
Irregular means the word does not follow a pattern. Irregular plurals need to be memorized.

Write the correct plural in each blank.

My mom is the smartest (woman, **women**) I've ever met. woman

Our babysitter Bobby picks up three (child, **children**) after school each day. children

Animal Plurals

Some animal names are the same in their singular and plural forms. There is one fish in the sea and there are five fish in the lake. Notice the yellow rows—those plurals are different!

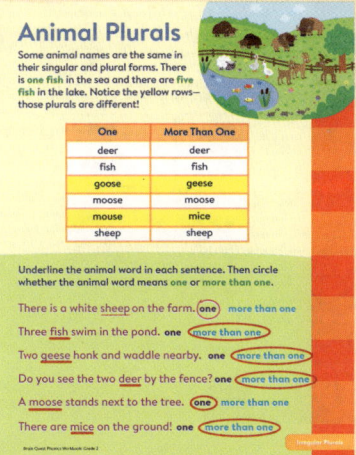

One	More Than One
deer	deer
fish	fish
goose	geese
moose	moose
mouse	mice
sheep	sheep

Underline the animal word in each sentence. Then circle whether the animal word means **one** or **more than one**.

There is a white sheep on the farm. **one** · more than one

Three fish swim in the pond. one · **more than one**

Two geese honk and waddle nearby. one · **more than one**

Do you see the two deer by the fence? one · **more than one**

A moose stands next to the tree. **one** · more than one

There are mice on the ground! one · **more than one**

Lots of Loaves

To make some words that end in **f** or **fe** plural, the ending letters are replaced with **ves**. The plural of **calf** is **calves**. The plural of **knife** is **knives**.

Write the plural of the singular noun to complete each sentence.

Two wolves chased the cat into a tree. wolf

So many leaves fell off the tree. leaf

It's a good thing a cat has nine lives ! life

Baker Bob baked so many loaves of bread. loaf

Let's split each loaf into halves . half

Where are the bread knives ? knife

BRAIN BOX
For words that end in **ff** like puff, just add **s** to make them plural. For some words that end in one **f**, like chef or brief, add an **s** to create the plurals chefs and briefs.

The two wives sat on the porch. wife

It was cold so they wore scarves . scarf

Two baby calves grazed in their yard. calf

An Irregular Match

Match the singular word to its plural.

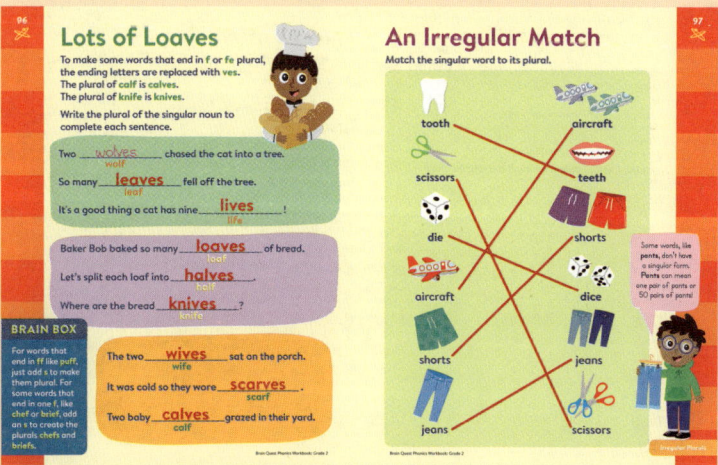

tooth → teeth
scissors → scissors
die → dice
aircraft → aircraft
shorts → shorts
jeans → jeans

aircraft
teeth
shorts
dice
jeans
scissors

Some words, like pants, don't have a singular form. Pants can mean one pair of pants or 50 pairs of pants!

Heroes to the Rescue

When words end in **o**, add **es** to make the word plural.

Add **es** to the ends of the words below to write the plural. Then write the word.

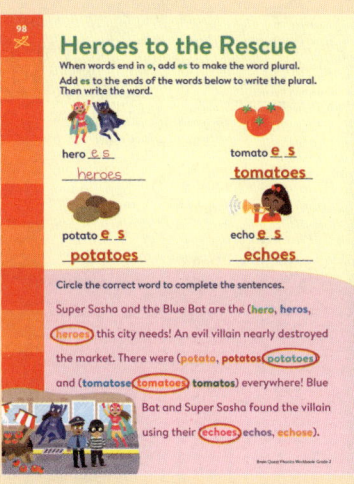

hero e s
heroes

tomato e s
tomatoes

potato e s
potatoes

echo e s
echoes

Circle the correct word to complete the sentences.

Super Sasha and the Blue Bat are the (hero, heros, **heroes**) this city needs! An evil villain nearly destroyed the market. There were (potato, potatos, **potatoes**) and (tomatose, **tomatoes**, tomatos) everywhere! Blue Bat and Super Sasha found the villain using their (**echoes**, echos, echose).

People in the Park

Write the singular or plural forms of the missing words.

Singular	Plural
child	children
person	people
woman	women
man	men
leaf	leaves
moose	moose
wolf	wolves
mouse	mice
goose	geese
sheep	sheep

Full of Gum

A **suffix** is a word ending that changes the word's meaning. The suffix **-ful** means "full of." **Cheerful** means "full of cheer." The suffix **-less** means "without." **Wireless** means "without wires."

Color the words with the suffix **-ful** blue.
Color the words with the suffix **-less** yellow.
Color the other words purple.

The suffixes **-ful** and **-less** have opposite meanings. **Joyful** and **joyless** use the same base word **joy** but have opposite meanings.

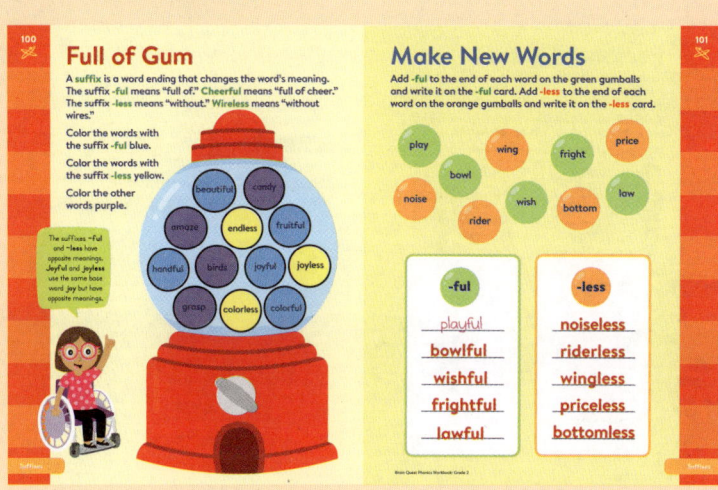

beautiful | candy
amaze | endless | fruitful
handful | birds | joyful | joyless
grasp | colorless | colorful

Make New Words

Add **-ful** to the end of each word on the green gumballs and write it on the **-ful** card. Add **-less** to the end of each word on the orange gumballs and write it on the **-less** card.

play | wing | fright | price
bowl | noise | wish | bottom | law
rider

-ful	-less
playful	noiseless
bowlful	riderless
wishful	wingless
frightful	priceless
lawful	bottomless

Pages 102–103

It's Cookie O'Clock

The prefix **pre-** means "before," like in **preset**. The prefix **mis-** means "wrongly," like in **misuse**.

Circle the correct prefix.

Then write the new word on the line.

To heat before is to __preheat__ . **pre / mis** heat

To hear wrongly is to __mishear__ . **pre / mis** hear

To pay before is to __prepay__ . **pre / mis** pay

To spell wrongly is to __misspell__ . **pre / mis** spell

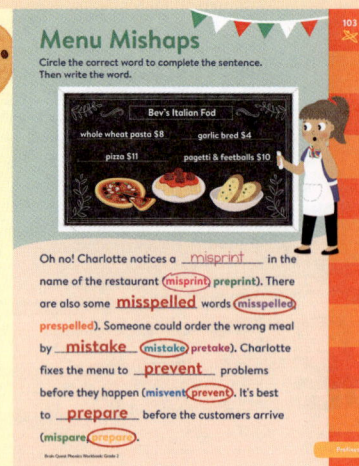

Menu Mishaps

Circle the correct word to complete the sentence. Then write the word.

Bev's Italian Fod
whole wheat pasta $8   garlic bred $4
pizza $11   pagetti & feetballs $10

Oh no! Charlotte notices a __misprint__ in the name of the restaurant (**misprint** / preprint). There are also some __misspelled__ words (**misspelled** / prespelled). Someone could order the wrong meal by __mistake__ (**mistake** / pretake). Charlotte fixes the menu to __prevent__ problems before they happen (misvent / **prevent**). It's best to __prepare__ before the customers arrive (mispare / **prepare**).

Page 104

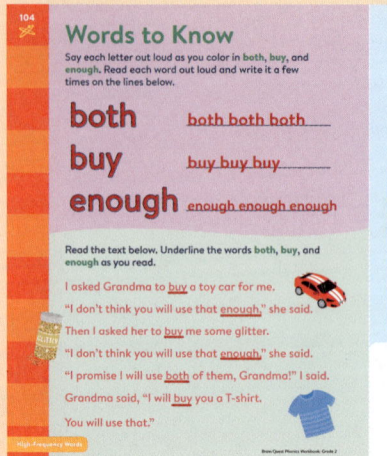

Words to Know

Say each letter out loud as you color in **both**, **buy**, and **enough**. Read each word out loud and write it a few times on the lines below.

both __both both both__

buy __buy buy buy__

enough __enough enough enough__

Read the text below. Underline the words **both**, **buy**, and **enough** as you read.

I asked Grandma to <u>buy</u> a toy car for me.

"I don't think you will use that <u>enough</u>," she said.

Then I asked her to <u>buy</u> me some glitter.

"I don't think you will use that <u>enough</u>," she said.

"I promise I will use <u>both</u> of them, Grandma!" I said.

Grandma said, "I will <u>buy</u> you a T-shirt. You will use that."

Page 107

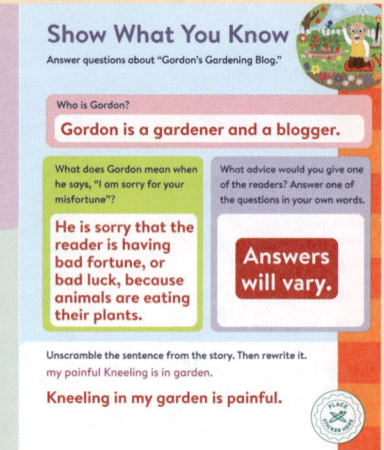

Show What You Know

Answer questions about "Gordon's Gardening Blog."

Who is Gordon?
Gordon is a gardener and a blogger.

What does Gordon mean when he says, "I am sorry for your misfortune"?
He is sorry that the reader is having bad fortune, or bad luck, because animals are eating their plants.

What advice would you give one of the readers? Answer one of the questions in your own words.
Answers will vary.

Unscramble the sentence from the story. Then rewrite it.
my painful Kneeling is in garden.
Kneeling in my garden is painful.

Pages 108–109

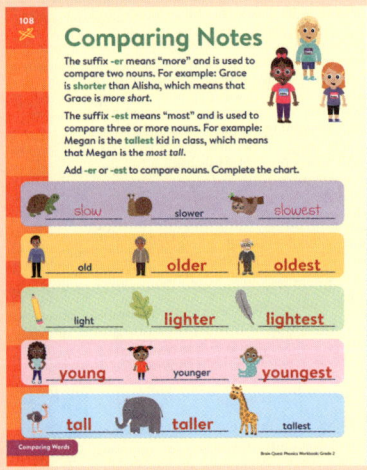

Comparing Notes

The suffix **-er** means "more" and is used to compare two nouns. For example: Grace is **shorter** than Alisha, which means that Grace is **more short**.

The suffix **-est** means "most" and is used to compare three or more nouns. For example: Megan is the **tallest** kid in class, which means that Megan is the **most tall**.

Add **-er** or **-est** to compare nouns. Complete the chart.

slow	slower	slowest
old	older	oldest
light	lighter	lightest
young	younger	youngest
tall	taller	tallest

Most of All

Write one word using **-er** or **-est** to replace the blue words in each sentence.

The white cake is the most plain cake of them all. __plainest__

Sam is the most small puppy in the litter. __smallest__

The sofa is more soft than the chair. __softer__

That flavor is the most gross I have ever tried. __grossest__

A jet would be the most quick way to get there. __quickest__

Nico felt more calm already. __calmer__

The cheetah is the most fast cat on earth. __fastest__

Pages 110–111

Cat Coins

The letter **c** makes two sounds: hard **c**, like in **cat**, and soft **c**, like in **cent**.

Say the word for each picture. Match the pictures to the box with the word that has the same beginning sound.

cat   **cent**

celery   crab   cloud   city   cake   camel

BRAIN BOX

When **c** is in front of an **i**, **y**, or **e**, it is soft and says /s/ like in **city**, **cycle**, and **race**. When **c** is in front of any other letter, it is hard and says /k/ like in **car**, **clam**, and **cone**.

Hard and Soft

The hard **c** sound can be in the middle or at the end of a word, or both, like in **picnic**.

The soft **c** sound can be the middle sound of a word, like in **acid**, or at the end, like in **price**.

Circle the word that has the same **c** sound as the picture.

music: face **act**   **pencil**: juice **secret**   **mice**: **police** cube

picnic: **hiccup** rice   **cup**: **uncle** braces   **lettuce**: ice **corn**

Color the clouds showing words that have both the soft **c** and hard **c** sounds.

circle   broccoli   device   arctic   cycle   crack   circus

Pages 112–113

Personal Titles

An **abbreviation** is a shortened form of a word. Titles like **Dr.** (doctor) and **Mr.** (mister) come before a person's name, like **Dr. Zuck** or **Mr. Chanin**.

Some titles, like **Jr.** (junior) and **Sr.** (senior), come after the name, like **Ken Griffey Sr.** and **Ken Griffey Jr.**

Match the personal title to the abbreviation.

Title	Abbreviation
Doctor	Esq.
Missus	Prof.
Junior	Hon.
Mister	Capt.
Senior	Mr.
Esquire	Sr.
Professor	Mrs.
Captain	Dr.
Honorable	Jr.

Ms. (say: mizz) is used before a woman's last name. It isn't short for another word. It is just Ms.!

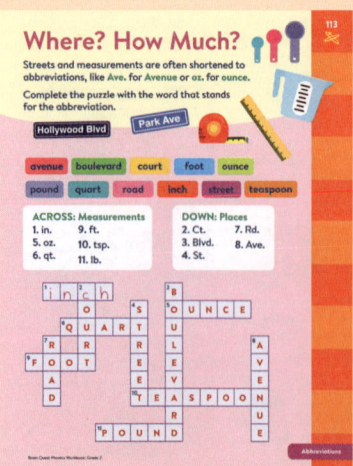

Where? How Much?

Streets and measurements are often shortened to abbreviations, like **Ave.** for **Avenue** or **oz.** for **ounce**.

Complete the puzzle with the word that stands for the abbreviation.

Hollywood Blvd   **Park Ave**

avenue   boulevard   court   foot   ounce   pound   quart   road   inch   street   teaspoon

ACROSS: Measurements
1. in.   9. ft.
5. oz.   10. tsp.
6. qt.   11. lb.

DOWN: Places
2. Ct.   7. Rd.
3. Blvd.   8. Ave.
4. St.

Pages 114–115

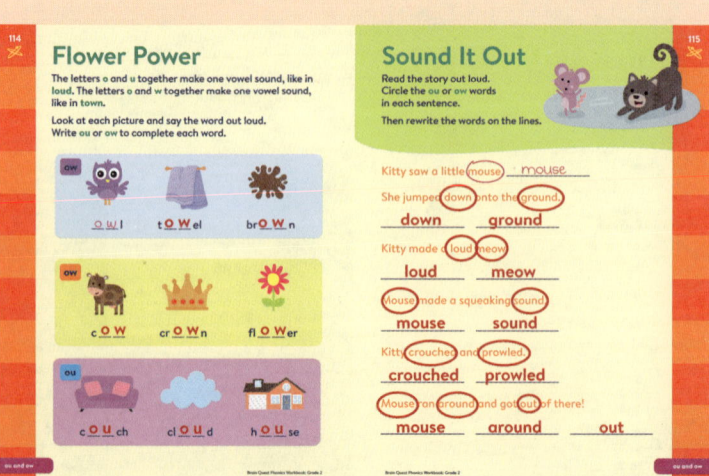

Flower Power

The letters **o** and **u** together make one vowel sound, like in **loud**. The letters **o** and **w** together make one vowel sound, like in **town**.

Look at each picture and say the word out loud. Write **ou** or **ow** to complete each word.

ow: o **W** l   t **O** wel   br **O** wn

ow: c **O** w   cr **O** wn   fl **O** wer

ou: c **O** ch   cl **O** ud   h **O** se

Sound It Out

Read the story out loud. Circle the **ou** or **ow** words in each sentence.

Then rewrite the words on the lines.

Kitty saw a little (mouse). __mouse__
She jumped (down) onto the (ground).
__down__   __ground__

Kitty made a (loud) (meow).
__loud__   __meow__

(Mouse) made a squeaking (sound).
__mouse__   __sound__

Kitty (crouched) and (prowled).
__crouched__   __prowled__

(Mouse) ran (around) and got (out) of there!
__mouse__   __around__   __out__

Pages 116–117

Page 120   Page 123

 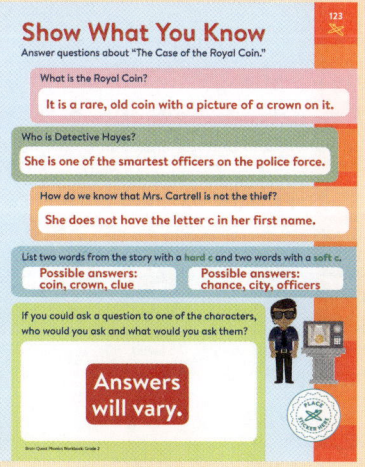

Pages 118–119

Pages 124–125

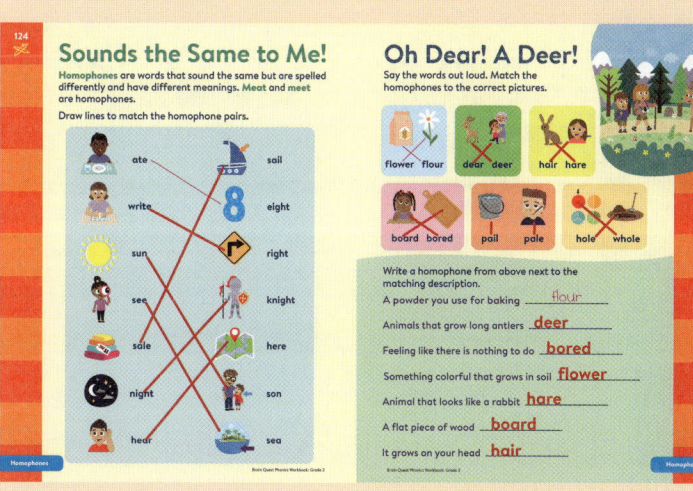

Pages 126–127

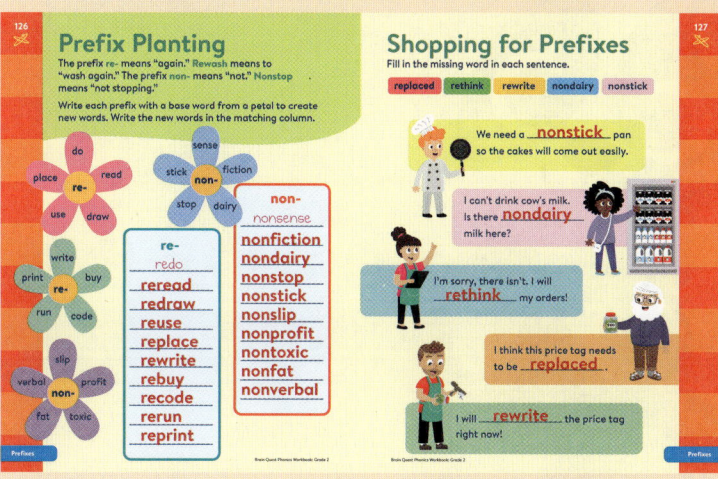

Pages 128–129

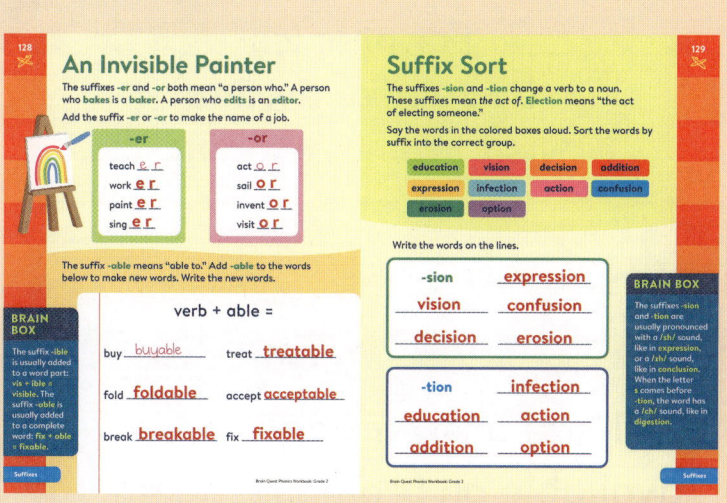

Brain Quest Phonics Workbook: Grade 2

Pages 130–131

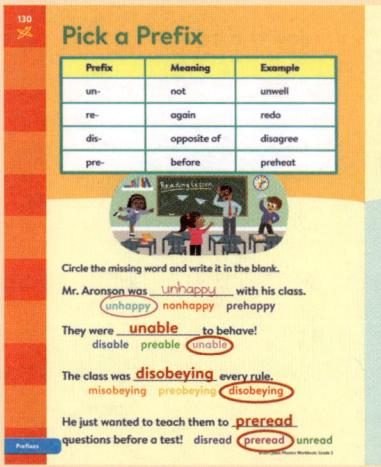

Pick a Prefix

Prefix	Meaning	Example
un-	not	unwell
re-	again	redo
dis-	opposite of	disagree
pre-	before	preheat

Circle the missing word and write it in the blank.

Mr. Aronson was __unhappy__ with his class.
(unhappy) nonhappy prehappy

They were __unable__ to behave!
disable preable (unable)

The class was __disobeying__ every rule.
misobeying preobeying (disobeying)

He just wanted to teach them to __preread__
questions before a test! disread (preread) unread

So Many Suffixes

Underline the suffix for each word in the example column.

Suffix	Meaning	Example
-ly	in a way that is	slowly
-er	more	funnier
-est	most	fastest
-er/-or	a person who	player

Circle the missing word and write it in the blank.

I love my Aunt Flor. She is the __nicest__ person in the world. nicer nicor (nicest)

She is __sillier__ than most people I know. silliest (sillier) sillyly

She is a __teacher__ for a second grade class.
teachor (teacher) teachest

Aunt Flor runs very __quickly__.
I can't beat her in a race!
quicky quickest (quickly)

Pages 132–133

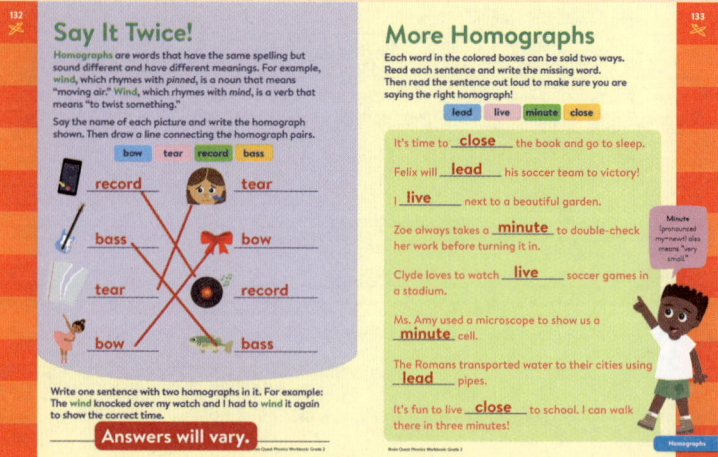

Say It Twice!

Homographs are words that have the same spelling but sound different and have different meanings. For example, wind, which rhymes with pinned, is a noun that means "moving air." Wind, which rhymes with mind, is a verb that means "to twist something."

Say the name of each picture and write the homograph shown. Then draw a line connecting the homograph pairs.

bow   tear   record   bass

record — tear
bass — bow
tear — record
bow — bass

Write one sentence with two homographs in it. For example: The wind knocked over my watch and I had to wind it again to show the correct time.

Answers will vary.

More Homographs

Each word in the colored boxes can be said two ways. Read each sentence and write the missing word. Then read the sentence out loud to make sure you are saying the right homograph!

lead   live   minute   close

It's time to __close__ the book and go to sleep.

Felix will __lead__ his soccer team to victory!

I __live__ next to a beautiful garden.

Zoe always takes a __minute__ to double-check her work before turning it in.

Clyde loves to watch __live__ soccer games in a stadium.

Ms. Amy used a microscope to show us a __minute__ cell.

The Romans transported water to their cities using __lead__ pipes.

It's fun to live __close__ to school. I can walk there in three minutes!

Pages 134–135

Put It Together

A contraction is a type of word that combines two or more words in a shortened form. For example, they're is a contraction for they are. Contractions use these punctuation marks ' called apostrophes.

I'm = I am
you're = you are
he's = he is
she's = she is
they'll = they will
we'll = we will

Circle the correct contraction to fill in the blank. Then write it on the line.

Heather said she would help me at 5:00 p.m. and __she's__ never late. you're (she's)

__I'm__ hoping that we can bake cookies together. (I'm) They'll

If Heather helps with the cookies, __they'll__ taste delicious. he's (they'll)

__We'll__ have fun together. We always do! (We'll) You're

BRAIN BOX
The apostrophe takes the place of the letters that drop out when words are written as contractions.

Contraction Action

can't = cannot
don't = do not
won't = will not
isn't = is not

Write the word or words that make up each contraction.

don't __do not__   isn't __is not__

can't __cannot__   won't __will not__

Read each sentence. Circle the word or words that could be rewritten with a contraction. Write the contraction on the line.

I (cannot) wait for the big day! __can't__

I (do not) want to spoil the surprise for my little brother. __don't__

He (is not) going to believe it. __isn't__

We are taking him on a trip to New York City that he (will not) forget. __won't__

Page 136

Words to Know

Say each letter out loud as you color in could, only, and right. Read each word out loud and write it a few times on the lines below.

could __could could could__

only __only only only__

right __right right right__

Write a word to fill in the blanks.

could   only   right

There are __only__ three days until we fly to California! I can't wait to sit in the sun __right__ under a palm tree. I __could__ spend every day like that. Maybe I will!

Page 139

Show What You Know

Answer questions about "Pirate Pete's Flea Market."

What are some things for sale at Pirate Pete's Flea Market?
__ropes, eye patches, clocks, pails, sails__

Why is Pirate Pete good at selling?
__Pirate Pete talks so much about the items in his shop that the shopper agrees to buy something to get him to stop.__

List three sets of words from the story that sound the same but have different spellings and meanings. **Answers include:**

I	eye
see	sea
sale	sail

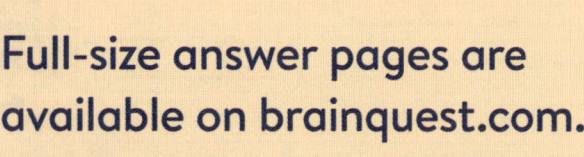

For phonics tips and activities, visit brainquest.com.

Full-size answer pages are available on brainquest.com.

QUESTIONS

Which word does NOT belong:
<u>stick</u>, <u>star</u>, <u>stone</u>, <u>short</u>?

Is the word for the item used to make calls spelled f–o–n–e or p–h–o–n–e?

Change the first letter of *wish* to make a word for an animal that lives in the water.

I tell time. My name rhymes with *block*. What am I?

BRAIN QUEST®

QUESTIONS

Which word has the same ending sounds as *ink*:
<u>luck</u> or <u>pink</u>?

I am worn on a finger. My name rhymes with *king*. What am I?

Change the first letter of *thin* to make a word for a part of the face.

Which is a large animal that lives in the ocean:
a <u>wail</u> or a <u>whale</u>?

BRAIN QUEST®

QUESTIONS

Which word has the same vowel sound as *use*:
<u>hole</u> or <u>huge</u>?

Spell the name of a black-and-white animal that is known for being stinky.

Which word has the same beginning sounds as *truck*:
<u>brick</u> or <u>trip</u>?

The blend in the word *stop* is *st*. True or false?

BRAIN QUEST

QUESTIONS

You use me when you go camping. My name rhymes with *bent*. What am I?

Which is part of a flower: a <u>steam</u> or a <u>stem</u>?

Put this sentence in order: "duck The pond in swims the."

Which word has the same ending sounds as *slug*:
<u>plug</u> or <u>ping</u>?

BRAIN QUEST®

QUESTIONS

In a blend, like *bl* or *spr*, you can hear all the letter sounds. True or false?

Change one letter in *dunk* to make a word for a kind of bird.

Which word has the same beginning sounds as *drum*:
<u>drip</u> or <u>green</u>?

I am at the playground. My name rhymes with *thing*. What am I?

BRAIN QUEST®

QUESTIONS

Is the word for the number after seven spelled a–t–e or e–i–g–h–t?

Which word has the same vowel sound as *shy*:
<u>bride</u> or <u>trick</u>?

Adding the letter *s* to the end of a verb shows that the action is happening now. True or false?

I am a boat, but bigger. My name rhymes with *whip*. What am I?

BRAIN QUEST

Brain Quest Mini-Deck

ANSWERS

short (*Short* begins with the digraph *sh*. The other words begin with the *st* blend.)

p–h–o–n–e (phone)

fish

a clock

BRAIN QUEST®

ANSWERS

pink

a ring

chin

a whale

BRAIN QUEST®

ANSWERS

huge (Both words have the long u sound.)

s–k–u–n–k (skunk)

trip

true

BRAIN QUEST®

ANSWERS

a tent

a stem

"The duck swims in the pond."

plug

BRAIN QUEST®

ANSWERS

true

duck

drip (Both words start with the *dr* blend.)

a swing

BRAIN QUEST®

ANSWERS

e–i–g–h–t (eight)

bride (Both words have the long i sound.)

true

a ship

BRAIN QUEST®

Brain Quest Mini-Deck

QUESTIONS

Which word has the short i sound: bite or bit?

Two words that have the same ending sound rhyme. True or false?

Is the word for something you wear when it's cold out spelled: c-o-t or c-o-a-t?

I am used to carry food. My name rhymes with *day*. What am I?

BRAIN QUEST®

QUESTIONS

Which word does NOT belong: hopped, swimming, walked, skipped?

Add a vowel to the end of *kit* to make a word for something that can fly in the sky.

Spell the word for what falls from the sky when it is really cold.

Which has the long e sound: ski or skin?

BRAIN QUEST®

QUESTIONS

Change the first letter in *funny* to make a word for a baby rabbit.

Which word does NOT belong: runs, jumped, swims, buys?

I am part of a foot. My name rhymes with *go*. What am I?

Which word has the long u sound: cub or cube?

BRAIN QUEST®

QUESTIONS

Which word is a verb in present tense: yawns or hills?

Find the blend in the word *broke*.

The words *they* and *weigh* rhyme. True or false?

Which word does NOT belong: drink, dump, draw, drum?

BRAIN QUEST®

QUESTIONS

Which word has the same vowel sound as *mule*: use or mug?

A noun is a word that shows action. True or false?

Unscramble these letters to make a word for a number: o-f-r-u

Find the verbs: "Tam runs to the stage and sings."

BRAIN QUEST®

QUESTIONS

Which word has the same vowel sound as *bird*: board or burp?

This word is the name of a color and the name of a fruit. What is it?

A past tense verb means that the action already happened. True or false?

Find the nouns: "The hippo opened its mouth."

BRAIN QUEST®

Brain Quest Mini-Deck

ANSWERS

bit (*Bite* has the long i sound.)

true

c–o–a–t (coat)

a tray

BRAIN QUEST

ANSWERS

swimming (*Swimming* is present tense. The other words are past tense.)

kite

s–n–o–w (snow)

ski (*Skin* has the short i sound.)

BRAIN QUEST

ANSWERS

bunny

jumped (*Jumped* is in the past tense. The other words are in present tense.)

a toe

cube (*Cub* has the short u sound.)

BRAIN QUEST

ANSWERS

yawns

br (broke)

true (*They* and *weigh* both end in the long a sound.)

dump (The other words begin with the *dr* blend.)

BRAIN QUEST

ANSWERS

use (Both words have the long u sound.)

false (A verb shows action. A noun names a person, place, or thing.)

f–o–u–r (four)

"Tam runs to the stage and sings."

BRAIN QUEST

ANSWERS

burp (Both words have the /er/ sound.)

orange

true

"The hippo opened its mouth."

BRAIN QUEST

QUESTIONS

Which word has the /f/ sound in it: <u>phone</u> or <u>choose</u>?

Which word does NOT belong: <u>say</u>, <u>train</u>, <u>hat</u>, <u>game</u>?

Find the verbs: "Jay turned and raced up the stairs."

Which word has the same vowel sound as *door*: <u>roar</u> or <u>dirt</u>?

BRAIN QUEST

QUESTIONS

I am a small bag that rhymes with *nurse*. What am I?

What does the suffix *-ing* mean?

More and *war* have the same vowel sound. True or false?

Change the verb to past tense: "The kitten crawls onto his lap."

BRAIN QUEST

QUESTIONS

What does the suffix *-ed* mean?

Spell the name for the long o word found in the center of an apple.

Find the verbs: "The group stands and holds hands."

Turtle and *her* have the same vowel sound. True or false?

BRAIN QUEST

QUESTIONS

Unscramble these letters to make a word for something that can be molded: a–l–y–c

What is the plural of *goose*?

Which word has the same vowel sound as *claim*: <u>clip</u> or <u>stray</u>?

Which sentence is in the past tense? "<u>The bug flies.</u>" or "<u>The bug flew.</u>"

BRAIN QUEST

QUESTIONS

Which word has the same vowel sound as *snail*: <u>gray</u> or <u>snack</u>?

Add *-ing* to the verb: "They are make dinner."

Which word starts with a blend: <u>stripe</u>, <u>short</u>, <u>sash</u>?

Which word is past tense: <u>copied</u> or <u>copies</u>?

BRAIN QUEST

QUESTIONS

Change the first letter of *pail* to make a word for something a dog wags.

Which sentence is in the present tense? "<u>Ben studies.</u>" or "Ben stu<u>died.</u>"

What word is the abbreviation *Mr.* short for?

Which word does NOT belong: <u>splash</u>, <u>spray</u>, <u>splat</u>, <u>splay</u>?

BRAIN QUEST

Brain Quest Mini-Deck

phone

hat (*Hat* has the short a sound. The other words have the long a sound.)

"Jay turned and raced up the stairs."

roar

BRAIN QUEST®

a purse

It means the action is happening right now.

true

"The kitten crawled onto his lap."

BRAIN QUEST®

It means the action took place in the past.

c–o–r–e (core)

"The group stands and holds hands."

true

BRAIN QUEST®

c–l–a–y (clay)

geese

stray (Both words have the long a sound.)

"The bug flew."

BRAIN QUEST®

gray (Both words have the long a sound.)

"They are making dinner."

stripe (*Short* starts with the digraph sh. *Sash* starts with the letter s.)

copied

BRAIN QUEST®

tail

"Ben studies."

Mister

spray (*Spray* begins with the spr blend. The other words begin with the spl blend.)

BRAIN QUEST®

Brain Quest Mini-Deck

QUESTIONS

Unscramble these letters to make a word for a sound pigs make:
k–o–n–i

A plural noun means there is only one. True or false?

What is another word for *yell* that rhymes with *stream*?

Which has the same vowel sound as *point*:
joke or joy?

BRAIN QUEST®

QUESTIONS

Which word has the short i sound:
pick or pie?

Put this sentence in order: "hands on dried She towel her the."

Which word is missing a silent b at the end:
clam, gem, crum?

Find the plural nouns: "Sam packed three shirts, two skirts, and one purse."

BRAIN QUEST®

QUESTIONS

In which sentence is the verb spelled correctly? "I am planning a party." or "I am planing a party."

Which word is the plural word for *bag*:
bags or bages?

Change the first letter of *hook* to make a word for something found at the library.

Which word has the same vowel sound as *foot*:
fool or look?

BRAIN QUEST®

QUESTIONS

Which word is missing a silent k at the beginning:
nook, nock, note?

Change the first letter of *tickle* to make a word for a crunchy green snack.

In which sentence is the verb spelled correctly? "They huged tightly." or "They hugged tightly."

Which word has the same vowel sound as *boom*:
moon or brook?

BRAIN QUEST®

QUESTIONS

Which word does NOT belong:
knock, spin, gnat, wrist?

I can be found on a door. My name rhymes with *candle*. What am I?

Is the word for the furniture you eat on spelled
t–a–b–e–l or t–a–b–l–e?

Which has the long o sound:
hop or hope?

BRAIN QUEST®

QUESTIONS

Which is plural:
mice or maze?

Unscramble these letters to make a word for a bird:
e–g–l–e–a

Which two words can be combined to make a compound word:
bath, pot, flower?

Find the verbs: "Benny skipped and clapped with joy."

BRAIN QUEST®

Brain Quest Phonics Workbook: Grade 2

Brain Quest Mini-Deck

ANSWERS

ANSWERS

o–i–n–k (oink)

false (A plural noun means there is more than one.)

scream

joy (Both words have the /oi/ sound.)

BRAIN QUEST

ANSWERS

pick (*Pie* has the long i sound.)

"She dried her hands on the towel."

crum<u>b</u>

"Sam packed three <u>shirts</u>, two <u>skirts</u>, and one purse."

BRAIN QUEST

ANSWERS

"I am <u>planning</u> a party."

bags

book

look

BRAIN QUEST

ANSWERS

<u>k</u>nock

pickle

"They <u>hugged</u> tightly."

moon

BRAIN QUEST

ANSWERS

spin (The other words have silent first letters.)

a handle

t–a–b–l–e (table)

hope (*Hop* has the short o sound.)

BRAIN QUEST

ANSWERS

mice (It means *more than one mouse.*)

e–a–g–l–e (eagle)

pot, flower
(flower + pot = flowerpot)

"Benny <u>skipped</u> and <u>clapped</u> with joy."

BRAIN QUEST

CERTIFICATE OF ACHIEVEMENT

Earned by

for completing all sections in the

BRAIN QUEST®

SECOND GRADE PHONICS WORKBOOK

No. 1

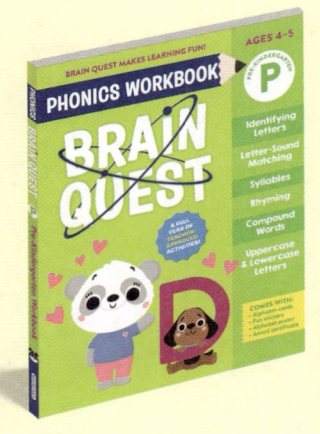
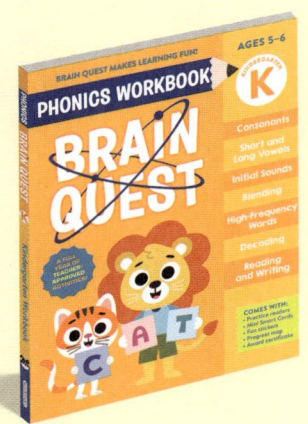
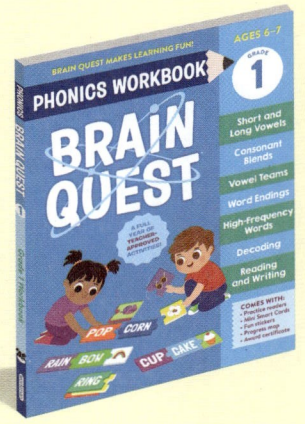
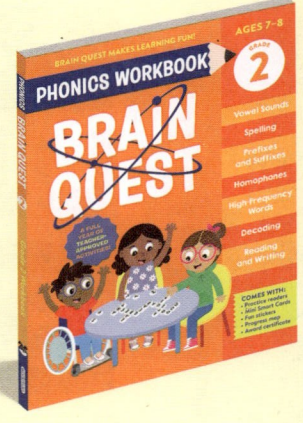

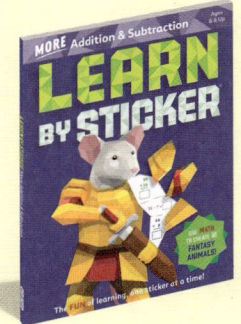

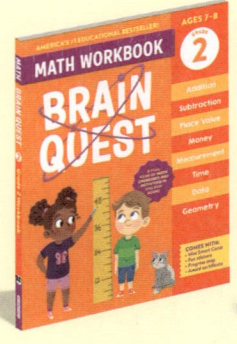

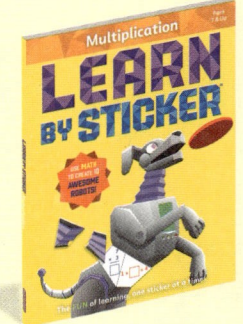
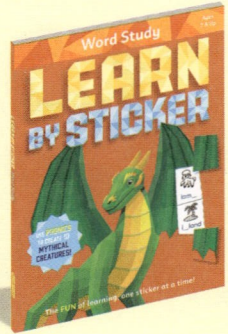

Ash and Liv at the Pond

Daytime/ Night Light

Which Wish Will Bernice Pick?

Fun Facts About Spruce Trees

Making Sparkle Cookies

Carnival Buzz

Gordon's Gardening Blog

The Case of the Royal Coin

Pirate Pete's Flea Market

I ♥ READING!

BOOK TIME!

PHONICS IS FUN

BRAINIAC

READING CHAMP

READER!

PHONICS WHIZ

BOOK TIME!

SHHH! I'M READING!

PHONICS IS FUN

BRAINIAC

PHONICS WHIZ

PHONICS WHIZ

I ♥ READING!

Proud reader!

Proud reader!

SHHH! I'M READING!

READER!

READING CHAMP